WARRIOR NOTES HOMESCHOOLING

New Testament Bible

Kindergarten

Units 3 & 4

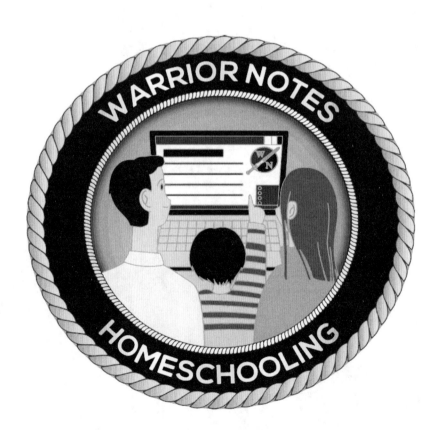

Warrior Notes Homeschooling

Kindergarten New Testament Bible

Focus: Value and Identity

Before every lesson, each child should pray a prayer so that their heart is ready to receive the word of God. We have provided a prayer for you to use, but you can use your own prayer if you like: "Lord God, prepare my heart so that it has fertile soil for the word of God to fall on, so that it will produce fruit in my life. Open my ears to hear your word and open my eyes to understand your word. In Jesus name, amen."

Every week has a new Bible verse, and the students are encouraged to memorize the verse of the week. Learning to memorize scriptures is a powerful way for young children to learn the Bible. Students will fill in the blank with the correct word or words missing from the weekly scripture verse.

Students will also be asked to learn at least one important thing from the week's lessons and tell you about it, write it down, and/or draw a picture about it for the weekly assessment.

Each lesson has an opening prayer, the Bible memory verse, What do you already know? (Where the student writes or tells what they already know about the topic. Examples will be given for the first two weeks. Students are encouraged to start to come up with their own answers by the third week.) What do you want to know, The Bible lesson and Something new that I learned today was. Students can write, draw, or say what they learned to their parent or guardian, but they are encouraged to draw a picture and explain to you what they have drawn.

Every so often throughout the lessons, you will see an underlined word. This word has been underlined because it will most likely need an explanation from an adult. An example from a lesson is the word repopulate. Just try your best to describe the underlined word, or you can look it up to find the definition.

We know that each child learns differently and at different paces. This being the case, the lessons are laid out in a day-to-day format in order to find consistency, but it is up to you as the parent/guardian to determine the actual pace and learning style of your child. You can go through the lessons faster or slower if you desire, depending on your child's level.

Opening Prayer

"Lord God prepare my heart so that it has fertile soil for the word of God to fall on so that it will produce fruit in my life. Open my ears to hear your word and open my eyes to understand your word. In Jesus name, amen."

Scope and Sequence (Outline):
Weeks 18-32 - 60 New Testament Bible lessons

Unit 3: New Testament lessons:
Week 18
Lesson 69-72: The young Jesus (About His Father's business)
Assessment
Week 19
Lesson 73-76: Jesus calls His disciples
Assessment
Week 20
Lesson 77-80: Jesus' many miracles
Assessment
Week 21
Lesson 81-82: The woman at the well
Lesson 83-84: Jesus sends out the disciples
Assessment
Week 22
Lesson 85-86: Jesus calms the storm
Lesson 87-88: Jesus continues to heal many
Assessment
Week 23
Lesson 89-90: Jesus feeds thousands of people
Lesson 91-92: The Transfiguration
Assessment
Week 24
Lesson 93-94:Jesus loves children
Lesson 95-96: Zacchaeus
Assessment
Week 25
Lesson 97-98:The good Samaritan
Lesson 99-100: The prodigal son
Assessment
Week 26
Lesson 101-102: Paul the apostle
Lesson 103-104: Paul talks to the Romans
Assessment
Week 27
Lesson 105-106: Paul talks to the Corinthians
Lesson 107-108: Paul talks to the Galatians
Assessment

Week 28
Lesson 109-110: Paul talks to the Ephesians
Lesson 111-112: Paul talks to the Philippians
Assessment
Week 29
Lesson 113-114: Paul talks to Timothy
Lesson 115-116: Hebrews
Assessment
Week 30
Lesson 117-118: James
Lesson 119-120: Peter
Assessment
Week 31
Lesson 121-122: John
Lesson 123-124: Revelation
Assessment

Unit 4: Holiday and special lessons:
Lesson 125: Birth of Jesus (Christmas)
Lesson 126: Jesus' triumphal entry (Palm Sunday)
Lesson 127: Christ's crucifixion and resurrection (Resurrection Sunday)
Lesson 128: Jesus is alive, and He returns to heaven (The Day of Pentecost and the sending of the promised Holy Spirit)

Unit 3: Lesson 69

Lesson Focus: The young Jesus

Opening prayer...

Bible Verse
Luke 2:40 (NKJV)
"And the Child grew and became strong in spirit, filled with wisdom; and the grace of God was upon Him."

What do you already know?

Jesus Bles Us

What do you want to know?

about Jesus.

Bible Lesson

The first part of the New Testament is called the Gospels. Each of the Gospels is about the life and ministry of Jesus, according to a different person. The book of Matthew is about the life and ministry of Jesus according to one of Jesus' disciples, Matthew. The Gospels start off by talking about the history of Jesus' family and his birth. Jesus' family history is from the <u>lineage</u> of King David and all the way back to Abraham. Jesus had earthly parents, but He was breathed into His mother's womb by the Holy Spirit before Jesus' mother and father were married. Jesus, God's Son, came down to the earth in the form of a baby. He came from heaven through a woman named Mary. This whole story about Jesus' birth is why we celebrate the Christian holiday of Christmas. Jesus' family was from a town called Nazareth, and His earthly father was a carpenter. Jesus was born in the city of Bethlehem and not in his hometown because Mary and Joseph, Jesus' earthly father, were traveling when He was born. There were prophecies in the Old Testament about a woman, who had not been with a man, giving birth to a son who would be called Immanuel, which means God with us. When Jesus was born, He fulfilled all of those Old Testament prophecies about Himself.

Something new that I learned today was:

mmanuel means God With us

Luke 2:40 (NKJV) "And the Child grew and became strong in spirit, filled with wisdom; and the grace of God was upon Him."

Write and Draw Box

Unit 3: Lesson 70

Lesson Focus: The young Jesus

Opening prayer...

Bible Verse
Luke 2:40 (NKJV)
"And the Child grew and became strong in spirit, filled with wisdom; and the grace of God was upon Him."

What do you already know?

mighty God Who he is

What do you want to know?

Bible Lesson

After Jesus was born in Bethlehem, God spoke to Joseph in a dream. He told Joseph to take his family to Egypt because King Herod felt threatened that another King was born and might take his place. King Herod wanted to find Jesus and kill Him, so Herod sent his soldiers out to kill all the babies in Bethlehem and the surrounding towns. Jesus and His family were not in the area, because they had been warned to flee to Egypt in a dream given to Joseph. Jesus began to grow as a young boy living in Egypt, fulfilling an Old Testament prophecy that God's Son would be called out of Egypt. Jesus and His family stayed in Egypt until the death of Herod so that they would be safe. When it was time for them to go back to their hometown, an angel of the Lord appeared to Joseph in a dream and told him that Herod was dead, and that they needed to go back to the land of Israel. When they neared their hometown, they realized that Herod's son was ruling over the land, and they wanted to make sure that Jesus stayed safe. After they were warned in another dream, they headed for their hometown city called Nazareth. They were going to fulfill the prophecy that said, "He shall be called a Nazarene."

Something new that I learned today was:

Luke 2:40 (NKJV) "And the Child grew and became strong in spirit, filled with wisdom; and the grace of God was upon Him."

Write and Draw Box

Testament Prophecy that God's

Who did God call out of Egypt? Jesus and His family stayed in Egypt until the death of

Unit 3: Lesson 71

Lesson Focus: The young Jesus

Opening prayer...

Bible Verse
Luke 2:40 (NKJV)
"And the Child grew and became strong in spirit, filled with wisdom; and the grace of God was upon Him."

What do you already know?

What do you want to know?

Bible Lesson

The Bible says, just like our memory verse talks about, Jesus grew and became strong in spirit, He was filled with wisdom, and His Father's grace was upon Him. Jesus grew up like any ordinary boy of His time. I am sure that He would often help His earthly father with his carpentry job. A son would often follow in his father's footsteps throughout history in whatever trade the father was in. Since Jesus' father was a carpenter, it is assumed that he also grew up learning His father's trade. As a carpenter, Jesus was most likely used to working with wood. He probably worked very hard for the family business. When Jesus was twelve years old, He went with His family to the feast of Passover. This feast of remembrance was celebrated in Jerusalem every year. When the feast was over, Jesus wanted to stay back in Jerusalem. At the same time, His family left the city to head back to their hometown. After traveling for a few days, Jesus' family realized that Jesus was not with them. They thought that Jesus had been traveling with some of His other relatives in the <u>caravan</u>. After they did not find Jesus among their other relatives, Jesus' family headed back to Jerusalem to find the young Jesus. They looked around the city for a while, and they finally found Jesus in the temple.

Herd

Something new that I learned today was:

Luke 2:40 (NKJV) "And the Child grew and became strong in spirit, filled with wisdom; and the grace of God was upon Him."

Write and Draw Box

Unit 3: Lesson 72

Lesson Focus: The young Jesus

Opening prayer...

Bible Verse
Luke 2:40 (NKJV)
"And the Child grew and became strong in spirit, filled with wisdom; and the grace of God was upon Him."

What do you already know?

What do you want to know?

Bible Lesson

When Jesus' family found him in the temple in Jerusalem, they found Him listening to the teachers and asking them questions. All the people there were amazed at the questions and answers that Jesus was giving to them in the temple. Jesus' mother and father went up to Jesus and asked Him, "Why have you done this to us? Why have you stayed here in Jerusalem while we all left the city?" Jesus' answer to them has amazed many for generations. He said to His family, "Did you not know that I needed to be doing my Father's business?" When Jesus said these things, His family did not really understand what He was saying to them. He was telling them that He needed to do the will of His heavenly Father. Jesus was not disobedient to his earthly parents, because the Bible says, "Children, obey your parents." Jesus was obeying His heavenly Father and doing the will of His heavenly Father. The scripture continues to tell us that Jesus was obedient to His parents, and He still grew in knowledge and wisdom after traveling back to His hometown of Nazareth. Jesus' mother kept all of the things that Jesus did within her heart. After all, an angel of the Lord did appear to Mary and Joseph, Jesus' parents, and told them that Mary would have a child that would be called the Son of God, "Son of the Highest; and the Lord God will give Him the throne of His father David, and He will reign over the house of Jacob forever, and of His kingdom, there will be no end." (Luke 1:32-33 NKJV)

Something new that I learned today was:

Luke 2:40 (NKJV) "And the Child grew and became strong in spirit, filled with wisdom; and the grace of God was upon Him."

Write and Draw Box

Unit 3 Week 18: Assessment

Lesson Focus: The young Jesus

Opening prayer...

Bible Verse: Write or tell the Bible verse to your parent.

Luke 2:40 (NKJV) "And the _____

grew and became _____

in spirit, filled with wisdom; and the grace of God

was upon Him."

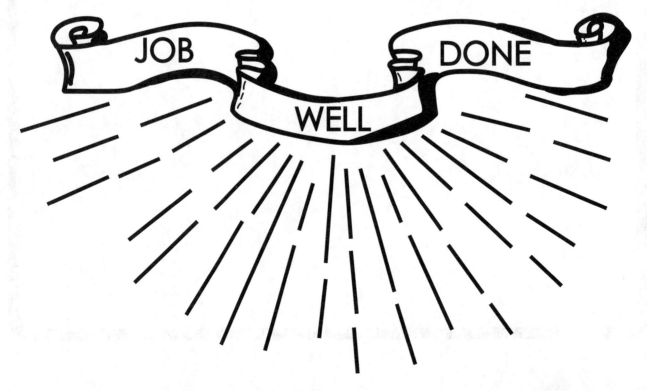

Write, draw or tell your parents what you learned this week. Talk about your favorite things.

Unit 3: Lesson 73

Lesson Focus: Jesus calls His disciples

Opening prayer...

Bible Verse
Matthew 4:17 (NKJV)
"From that time Jesus began to preach and to say, "Repent, for the kingdom of heaven is at hand."

What do you already know?

What do you want to know?

Bible Lesson

When Jesus was about thirty years old, He went to see His cousin John who was baptizing people and preaching <u>repentance</u>. John did not want to baptize Jesus at first because he thought he should be baptized by Jesus. As John was baptizing Jesus, heaven opened up, and the Holy Spirit came down in the form of what looked like a dove and came upon Him. The Holy Spirit is a person and not a bird. Then a voice from heaven said, "This is my Son, with who I am well pleased." Jesus began His ministry when He was about thirty years old. After He was baptized by John, He was led by the Spirit into the wilderness to be tempted by satan. After overcoming the temptations of satan and fasting for forty days, Jesus came out of the wilderness ready to start His ministry. Jesus was filled with the Spirit, and He went around ministering in many different towns and villages. Jesus preached the same message that John had preached, "Repent, for the kingdom of heaven is near." Jesus went to His hometown to go to the temple because that was a normal thing to do. He was handed the scroll of scripture to read, and it was from Isaiah. Jesus read, "The Spirit of the LORD is upon Me because He has anointed Me to preach the gospel to the poor...," and after Jesus was done reading, He closed up the scroll. He said, "Today, this scripture is fulfilled in your hearing." Jesus was saying to them that the prophecy in Isaiah was about Him. They said, "Who is this man to say these things, is He not the son of Joseph?"

Something new that I learned today was:

Matthew 4:17 (NKJV) "From that time Jesus began to preach and to say, "Repent, for the kingdom of heaven is at hand."

Write and Draw Box

Unit 3: Lesson 74

Lesson Focus: Jesus calls His disciples

Opening prayer...

Bible Verse
Matthew 4:17 (NKJV)
"From that time Jesus began to preach and to say, "Repent, for the kingdom of heaven is at hand."

What do you already know?

What do you want to know?

Bible Lesson

After Jesus spoke in His hometown and said that the scriptures were talking about Him, the townspeople all gathered together to take Him out to the edge of the city to throw Him off of a cliff. Knowing what they planned to do, Jesus walked right through the crowd and back to the town. Jesus was walking by the Sea of Galilee, and He saw two brothers there who were fishermen. He called to them and said, "Follow Me, and I will make you fishers of men." The two men, **Peter and Andrew**, instantly followed after Jesus and left their boats and nets behind. We must use this as an example today. When Jesus calls us to do something, we must instantly obey and do what He says. Our obedience is the key to seeing Him move in power in our lives. Jesus was still walking along by the Sea of Galilee, and He saw two more brothers who were fishermen, who were with their father, mending their fishing nets in their boat. Jesus called out to them like He did with the other two men and asked them to follow Him. Right away, the two brothers, **James and John**, the sons of Zebedee, followed Jesus. Jesus had already been ministering throughout the area before He went and called His disciples. He was in His hometown area when He called to them to follow Him. News of Jesus had spread throughout the region. Many people were amazed at what He was preaching and doing, or they were angry with Him and wanted to kill Him. The Bible says that Jesus could not do many miracles in His hometown because the people could not look past that He was just the son of Joseph and Mary. Jesus, equated Himself many times with God, His heavenly Father. This is why so many people wanted to kill Jesus. He was making Himself equal with God, the Creator of the universe.

Something new that I learned today was:

Matthew 4:17 (NKJV) "From that time Jesus began to preach and to say, "Repent, for the kingdom of heaven is at hand."

Write and Draw Box

Unit 3: Lesson 75

Lesson Focus: Jesus calls His disciples

Opening prayer...

Bible Verse
Matthew 4:17 (NKJV)
"From that time Jesus began to preach and to say, "Repent, for the kingdom of heaven is at hand."

What do you already know?

What do you want to know?

Bible Lesson

Jesus went around teaching and healing many people. Jesus had just sailed across the sea, and when He got off the boat, He saw a man who was paralyzed. Jesus said to the man, "Your sins are forgiven." Many who were there following Him and those watching Him said, "Who is this man who says that He can forgive sins?" Jesus, knowing their thoughts, said to them, "Which is easier to do, say your sins are forgiven, or to say take up your mat and walk?" Jesus, showing them that He had the power to do both, told the man to take up his mat and walk, and he did. Many people marveled at the miracles that Jesus did. Jesus went from there and saw a tax collector named **Matthew**, and He called to him to follow Him. Matthew rose up and followed Him. After this, Jesus saw a great crowd of people following Him, and He told those disciples who were with Him, "The harvest is plentiful, but the workers are few. Therefore, pray that the Lord of the harvest send out laborers." There were some of Jesus' disciples who were closer to Him than others who were following Him. This is because they chose to get closer to Jesus. We can choose how close we want to get to Jesus. Jesus also chose **Philip and Bartholomew**, as well as **Thomas**. Jesus then selected another **James**, the son of Alphaeus, **Thaddaeus, Simon the Canaanite**, and **Judas Iscariot**, who also betrayed Him. Jesus chose twelve of His disciples, who would also be called apostles. These twelve would follow Him everywhere He went and would later write about their time spent with Jesus.

Something new that I learned today was:

Matthew 4:17 (NKJV) "From that time Jesus began to preach and to say, "Repent, for the kingdom of heaven is at hand."

Write and Draw Box

Unit 3: Lesson 76

Lesson Focus: Jesus calls His disciples

Opening prayer...

Bible Verse
Matthew 4:17 (NKJV)
"From that time Jesus began to preach and to say, "Repent, for the kingdom of heaven is at hand."

What do you already know?

What do you want to know?

Bible Lesson

The twelve disciples were with Jesus when He performed many miracles, signs, and wonders. The disciples learned many things from their Master Teacher, Jesus. Jesus prayed over His disciples and said, "Wherever you go, preach, saying, 'The kingdom of heaven is at hand.' Heal the sick, cleanse the lepers, raise the dead, cast out demons. Freely you have received, freely give." Remember, John the baptizer preached this message. Jesus took up the message and preached it also, then He told His disciples that when they would go, they were to preach this message as well. Jesus also went on to say to them, "I send you out as sheep in the midst of wolves; therefore, be as wise as serpents and harmless as doves." Jesus told them to use wisdom but to be open to what the Lord had for them to do and say. Jesus also told them that they should not worry about what to say to others because the Spirit of the Father would speak through them to others. We can learn so much from this today. We use wisdom and study the word of God, and then when we go out among the people of the world, the Holy Spirit will give us the words to say. We do not have to worry about what we should say to others. He will speak through you to others when the time comes. Just have an open heart and be a willing vessel for His use. He loves you and has an excellent plan for you today. You are one of His disciples.

Something new that I learned today was:

Matthew 4:17 (NKJV) "From that time Jesus began to preach and to say, "Repent, for the kingdom of heaven is at hand."

Write and Draw Box

Unit 3 Week 19: Assessment

Lesson Focus: Jesus calls His disciples

Opening prayer...

Bible Verse: Write or tell the Bible verse to your parent.

Matthew 4:17 (NKJV)

"From that time _____ began to _____ and to say, "_____, for the kingdom of heaven is at hand."

Write, draw or tell your parents what you learned this week. Talk about your favorite things.

Unit 3: Lesson 77

Lesson Focus: Jesus' many miracles

Opening prayer...

Bible Verse

Matthew 4:23 (NKJV) "And Jesus went about all Galilee, teaching in their synagogues, preaching the gospel of the kingdom, and healing all kinds of sickness and all kinds of disease among the people."

What do you already know?

What do you want to know?

Bible Lesson

When Jesus started his ministry, after He was filled with the Holy Spirit, He went around all throughout the land of Galilee, healing all who were sick and demon-possessed. The first miracle in the Bible that Jesus performed was at a wedding. Jesus' mother was there, and someone told her that they had run out of wine. Jesus' mother told Jesus about it, and He said to her, "What does your concern have to do with me? My time has not yet come." Jesus' mother knew that Jesus could do something about the wine being all gone. Jesus honored his mother and did what she had asked of Him. Jesus told the servants at the wedding to fill all of the empty water jugs with water. They filled six waterpots with water, and Jesus told them to scoop some out and take it to their master. When they scooped it out, the water had turned into wine; Jesus had performed His first miracle. The Bible says that Jesus manifested His glory there in Galilee by doing this. His disciples followed Him and believed in Him from that day forward. The disciples believed in Jesus because they were there and witnessed His great miracles and healings. Jesus was a real man that lived on the earth. Today, we do not physically see Jesus on the earth like the disciples did as He performed many great signs, wonders, and miracles. So, the Bible tells us, we are blessed because we believe and have not seen. We can see more mighty miracles, signs, and wonders of Jesus today because Jesus is still alive, sitting at the right hand of His Father. He works through us, His believers, and all we have to do is believe and obey when He tells us to pray for sick people. He is the same God, yesterday, today, and forever.

Something new that I learned today was:

Matthew 4:23 (NKJV) "And Jesus went about all Galilee, teaching in their synagogues, preaching the gospel of the kingdom, and healing all kinds of sickness and all kinds of disease among the people."

Write and Draw Box

Unit 3: Lesson 78

Lesson Focus: Jesus' many miracles

Opening prayer...

Bible Verse

Matthew 4:23 (NKJV) "And Jesus went about all Galilee, teaching in their synagogues, preaching the gospel of the kingdom, and healing all kinds of sickness and all kinds of disease among the people."

What do you already know?

What do you want to know?

Bible Lesson

One of Jesus' first known public miracles was when a man with the disease of leprosy came to Him to be healed. The man said to Jesus, "If you are willing, you can make me clean." The man had faith that Jesus could cleanse and heal him. The word cleanse is used here because when someone has the disease of leprosy, they cannot be around other people because they are unclean. Other people can get the disease from them easily, if touched by them. Jesus said to the man, "I am willing, be cleansed." From that moment on, the man was healed of his leprosy. Jesus told him not to tell anyone about it, though, because His time had not yet come for His ministry to be launched out into the public. Jesus had <u>compassion</u> for the man. Jesus told the man that he needed to go and show himself to the priests as a part of the cleansing process, and to offer a gift to the Lord for his cleansing. A soldier called a centurion, who had a servant who was paralyzed and in great pain, came before Jesus and asked Him to heal his servant. Jesus agreed to go to the soldier's home, but the soldier told Jesus that He did not need to come to his home. He knew that Jesus just needed to speak the words and the servant would be made well. The soldier knew about authority because he was in charge of 100 soldiers. He could tell another soldier to go do something, and he would go. He knew that Jesus had authority like he did. Jesus <u>marveled</u> at the soldier's faith and told him that it would be done as he believed. From that moment, his servant was made well.

Something new that I learned today was:

Matthew 4:23 (NKJV) "And Jesus went about all Galilee, teaching in their synagogues, preaching the gospel of the kingdom, and healing all kinds of sickness and all kinds of disease among the people."

Write and Draw Box

Unit 3: Lesson 79

Lesson Focus: Jesus' many miracles

Opening prayer...

Bible Verse

Matthew 4:23 (NKJV) "And Jesus went about all Galilee, teaching in their synagogues, preaching the gospel of the kingdom, and healing all kinds of sickness and all kinds of disease among the people."

What do you already know?

What do you want to know?

Bible Lesson

Jesus went to Peter's house, and Peter's mother was sick with a fever. Jesus touched her hand, she was healed, and she served them. Later that evening, many sick people were brought to Him, and He healed them all. Demon-possessed people were also brought to Him, and they were set free from the demons. When Jesus did all of these things, He was fulfilling prophecy about Himself because the Bible says, "He Himself took our infirmities, and bore our sicknesses." (Isaiah 53:4 NKJV) Jesus had crossed over the sea of Galilee, and the people there brought Him a man who was paralyzed. Jesus saw the people's faith, and He said to the man, "Your sins are forgiven." The religious people who heard Him said that He was blaspheming God by saying that He could forgive sins. When Jesus said this, He was making Himself equal to God. The people only knew Him as the son of Joseph and Mary and not God's Son. Jesus knew their thoughts and said to them, "So that you know that I have the power to forgive sins," and He told the man to rise up and walk. When the paralyzed man stood up and walked, the people who were watching were filled with awe and wonder, and they glorified God. We can learn from these stories that Jesus heals, and He is the same yesterday, today, and forever. He has not changed, and He still heals today. Jesus wants everyone to be healedListen to the voice of the Lord as He speaks to you about praying for the sick and obey His voice. Pray for those who are sick and those who have demons. God will use you. Do not let anyone tell you that God cannot use you because you are young.

Something new that I learned today was:

Matthew 4:23 (NKJV) "And Jesus went about all Galilee, teaching in their synagogues, preaching the gospel of the kingdom, and healing all kinds of sickness and all kinds of disease among the people."

Write and Draw Box

Unit 3: Lesson 80

Lesson Focus: Jesus' many miracles

Opening prayer...

Bible Verse

Matthew 4:23 (NKJV) "And Jesus went about all Galilee, teaching in their synagogues, preaching the gospel of the kingdom, and healing all kinds of sickness and all kinds of disease among the people."

What do you already know?

What do you want to know?

Bible Lesson

Two blind men were calling out to Jesus as He was passing by them, "Son of David, have mercy on us!" By saying this, they were stating that Jesus was the long-awaited Messiah that the Old Testament prophecies talked about. This Messiah would be a descendant of David, which Jesus was. Jesus did have the right to be an earthly king as well as the heavenly King that He was. His disciples had an idea of what they thought Jesus would do as the long-awaited Messiah. They believed that Jesus would march with them into Jerusalem and proclaim Himself as the next earthly king. This is why they did not fully understand when Jesus said that He had to die. Jesus asked the blind men if they thought that He was able to heal them. They said "Yes," and He said to them, "Let it be done to you, according to your faith." They were healed at that moment. There was a man named Lazarus who was sick and had died. Jesus loved this family, but He stayed in a town ministering to people when Lazarus was sick. Jesus could have gone and healed him when he was sick. Instead, He waited until Lazarus had died to go to the family so that the people could see the power of God. Jesus went to their home, and the family was all there crying because Lazarus was dead. Jesus told them that he would rise again. Jesus went to the place where he was buried and called him to come out. Lazarus came out of the grave, and the people all believed in Jesus' power and authority.

Something new that I learned today was:

Matthew 4:23 (NKJV) "And Jesus went about all Galilee, teaching in their synagogues, preaching the gospel of the kingdom, and healing all kinds of sickness and all kinds of disease among the people."

Write and Draw Box

Unit 3 Week 20: Assessment

Lesson Focus: Jesus' many miracles

Opening prayer...

Bible Verse: Write or tell the Bible verse to your parent.

Matthew 4:23 (NKJV) "And Jesus went about all _____, teaching in their synagogues, preaching the gospel of the kingdom, and _____ all kinds of _____ and all kinds of disease among the people."

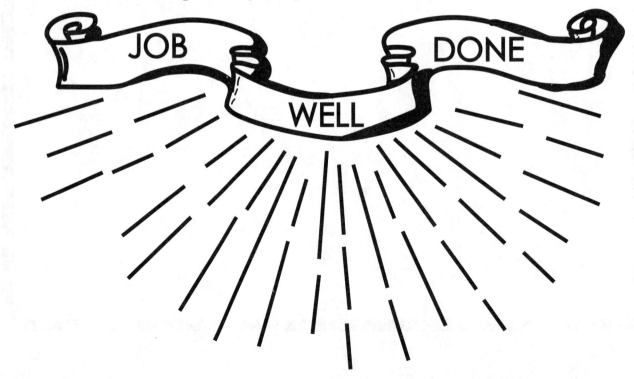

Write, draw or tell your parents what you learned this week. Talk about your favorite things.

Unit 3: Lesson 81

Lesson Focus: The woman at the well

Opening prayer...

Bible Verse
John 4:7 (NKJV)
"A woman of Samaria came to draw water. Jesus said to her, "Give Me a drink."

What do you already know?

What do you want to know?

Bible Lesson

There was a well that was called Jacob's well, where people would stop and get some water. Jesus was on a journey, and the Bible says that He was <u>wearied</u> from his trip. He sat down there by the well. A Samaritan woman came to get some water, and He asked her for a drink because His disciples were not with Him to help Him. The woman wondered why Jesus had asked her for a drink because Jews did not associate with Samaritans. Jesus told her that if she only knew who was asking her for a drink, she would have asked Him for Living Water. She wondered what Jesus was saying to her because she said to him, "Are you greater than our father Jacob who gave us this well to drink from?" Jesus replied to her and told her, "Whoever drinks from this well will be thirsty again, but whoever drinks of the water that I will give them will never thirst again." The woman was still thinking about earthly things as Jesus was talking about spiritual things. The woman said to Jesus, "Give me some of this water so that I do not have to keep coming back to this well to take water out again and again." Jesus was trying to tell her that He was the Living Water and that she should realize that He was the Messiah. Today, we can learn that Jesus has living water for us, and when we drink from Him each day, we will not thirst again. Spend time with Jesus today. He will give you His living water.

Something new that I learned today was:

John 4:7 (NKJV) "A woman of Samaria came to draw water. Jesus said to her, "Give Me a drink."

Write and Draw Box

Unit 3: Lesson 82

Lesson Focus: The woman at the well

Opening prayer...

Bible Verse
John 4:7 (NKJV)
"A woman of Samaria came to draw water. Jesus said to her, "Give Me a drink."

What do you already know?

What do you want to know?

Bible Lesson

Jesus told the woman at the well to go and get her husband and come back. She said "I have no husband." Jesus replied to her, "It is true you do not have one husband, you have had five husbands, and the one you are with now is not your husband." The woman told Jesus that He was a prophet for telling her about her life. The woman said to Jesus, "The Jews say that we should worship God in Jerusalem, but our fathers worshipped God on this mountain." Jesus said to her, "The time is coming when people will neither worship in Jerusalem or on the mountain. True worshipers will worship God in spirit and in truth." God is Spirit, and those who worship Him must worship Him in spirit and in truth. The woman said to Jesus, "I know that the Christ is coming soon, and He will tell us all these things." Jesus said to the woman, "I who speak to you, am He." What a powerful moment this must have been. Jesus the Messiah just told the woman at the well that He was the long-awaited Messiah that she was speaking of. The woman went into the city and told all the people she could find about the man at the well who knew everything she had ever done. She said to the people, "Could this be the Messiah?" Many people went out to see Jesus, and many believed in Jesus that day. We must worship Him in spirit and in truth. He is a spirit, and we must worship Him in spirit. People often worship God with their soul and body, but they do not worship Him with their spirit.

Something new that I learned today was:

John 4:7 (NKJV) "A woman of Samaria came to draw water. Jesus said to her, "Give Me a drink."

Write and Draw Box

Unit 3: Lesson 83

Lesson Focus: Jesus sends out the disciples

Opening prayer...

Bible Verse

Matthew 10:7-8 (NKJV) "And as you go, preach, saying, 'The kingdom of heaven is at hand.' Heal the sick, cleanse the lepers, raise the dead, cast out demons. Freely you have received, freely give."

What do you already know?

What do you want to know?

Bible Lesson

Jesus gathered all twelve disciples together and gave them authority to heal the sick, cast out demons, and raise the dead. Jesus told them that when they went out, they must preach, "The kingdom of heaven is at hand." Jesus poured into them and taught them what he knew, and they saw Jesus perform many miracles. Jesus told them to go and do the same things that He did. Jesus said they were not supposed to take any money with them because God would provide for them as they went. Jesus even told them that they were not supposed to take any extra clothes, shoes, or head coverings with them because a workman is worthy of his hire. This means that if the disciples preached and taught the people, they should help clothe and feed them if needed. Jesus also told them that when they came to a house, if they were welcomed, they were to bless the house and let their peace be upon it. If a household did not accept them, they were not to leave their peace at that house, and they were to shake off the dust from their sandals and have nothing to do with that city. Jesus said that it would be better for Sodom and Gomorrah on the day of judgment than for them. We can learn today that God will provide for us when we go and do His will.

Something new that I learned today was:

Matthew 10:7-8 (NKJV) "And as you go, preach, saying, 'The kingdom of heaven is at hand.' 8 Heal the sick, cleanse the lepers, raise the dead, cast out demons. Freely you have received, freely give."

Write and Draw Box

Unit 3: Lesson 84

Lesson Focus: Jesus sends out the disciples

Opening prayer...

Bible Verse

Matthew 10:7-8 (NKJV) "And as you go, preach, saying, 'The kingdom of heaven is at hand.' Heal the sick, cleanse the lepers, raise the dead, cast out demons. Freely you have received, freely give."

What do you already know?

What do you want to know?

Bible Lesson

Jesus went on to tell the disciples that He was sending them out as sheep among wolves. They were to be as wise as serpents and as harmless as doves as they went. Jesus warned them that they would be brought before men to testify to why they were preaching. They were not supposed to worry about what they would say at that time, because the Holy Spirit would give them the words to say. It is not you who speak, but the Spirit of the Father within you who speaks through you. What we can learn from this is that we do not need to worry about what to say to others; the Holy Spirit will always speak through us. Jesus went on to say that they would be hated for His name's sake and that those who endure to the end will be saved. Jesus told them that they were to flee to another town if they were persecuted in one city. There would be enough cities for them to go to until the Lord came back. Jesus also said to them, "A disciple is not above his teacher." If people persecuted Jesus, people would also persecute them for what they did. Today, we can learn that we will also be persecuted for our beliefs because Jesus was persecuted for His preaching and beliefs, and we are not above our Master.

Something new that I learned today was:

Matthew 10:7-8 (NKJV) "And as you go, preach, saying, 'The kingdom of heaven is at hand.' 8 Heal the sick, cleanse the lepers, raise the dead, cast out demons. Freely you have received, freely give."

Write and Draw Box

Unit 3 Week 21: Assessment

Lesson Focus: Jesus sends out the disciples

Opening prayer...

Bible Verse: Write or tell the Bible verse to your parent.

Matthew 10:7-8 (NKJV) "And as you go, _____, saying, 'The kingdom of _____ is at hand.' Heal the sick, cleanse the lepers, raise the dead, cast out _____. Freely you have received, freely give."

Write, draw or tell your parents what you learned this week. Talk about your favorite things.

Unit 3: Lesson 85

Lesson Focus: Jesus calms the storm

Opening prayer...

Bible Verse
Luke 8:24b (NKJV)

"Then He arose and rebuked the wind and the raging of the water. And they ceased, and there was a calm."

What do you already know?

What do you want to know?

Bible Lesson

Jesus wanted to go to the other side of the lake, so he told His disciples to get the boat ready. They all entered the boat, and Jesus fell asleep. As Jesus was sleeping in the ship's stern, a great storm arose in the lake, causing the wind and the waves to be very high. There was a lot of water coming into the boat because of the storm, and the disciples had to try to get as much of the water out of the boat as possible because they did not want to sink. They went to Jesus while all of this was happening and said to Him, "Master, wake up, don't you care if we all die out here in this storm?" Jesus woke up, and He rebuked the wind and the waves, and right away, the lake was calm again. Jesus said to the disciples, "Where is your faith?" The disciples could not believe their eyes. Even the wind and the waves obeyed Jesus. They were afraid, and they marveled at Jesus because of these things. Very shortly after they witnessed Jesus calm the storm, they reached the other side of the lake. Jesus got out of the boat, and He was met there by a man who had evil spirits, who lived among the tombs. When the demons saw Jesus, they said, "What do you want with us, Jesus? Do not torment us." Jesus asked him what his name was, and he said "legion," because many demons had entered into the man. Jesus commanded the evil spirits to leave the man, and they asked if they could go into some nearby pigs, and he allowed them. The pigs all ran off a cliff nearby and drowned. Jesus and the disciples got into the boat and headed back to the other side of the lake again.

Something new that I learned today was:

Luke 8:24b (NKJV) "Then He arose and rebuked the wind and the raging of the water. And they ceased, and there was a calm."

Write and Draw Box

Unit 3: Lesson 86

Lesson Focus: Jesus calms the storm

Opening prayer...

Bible Verse
Luke 8:24b (NKJV)
"Then He arose and rebuked the wind and the raging of the water. And they ceased, and there was a calm."

What do you already know?

What do you want to know?

Bible Lesson

Jesus wanted to go and be by Himself because he had heard about the death of His cousin John. After Jesus dismissed the great crowds of people who were there listening to Him teach, He went to be alone and pray up on the mountain. He sent the disciples ahead to go across the sea. The disciples got into a boat and headed toward the other side of the sea, when a great storm arose and the wind and the waves were very high. The Bible says that the ship was near the middle of the sea and at about the fourth watch of the night. Jesus saw the disciples really working hard to try to paddle the boat in the storm. Jesus went out to them, walking on the water. He thought about passing them by when one of them saw Jesus and was scared because he felt that He was a ghost. Instantly, Jesus called out to them and said, "It is just me, Jesus, no need to worry!" Peter was unsure if it was really Jesus, and he said, "If it is really you Jesus, tell me to come to you on the water." Jesus told him to come to Him. Peter stepped out of the boat and began to walk on the water. As he took his eyes off of Jesus and started to be concerned about the storm around him, he fell into the sea and began to sink. He cried out to Jesus, "Lord save me!" and Jesus reached out and grabbed him and took him back to the boat. He said to Peter, "Oh you of little faith; why did you doubt?" As soon as Jesus entered the boat, the wind and waves calmed down. Those who were in the boat worshiped Him, saying, "Truly you are the Son of God."

Something new that I learned today was:

Luke 8:24b (NKJV) "Then He arose and rebuked the wind and the raging of the water. And they ceased, and there was a calm."

Write and Draw Box

Unit 3: Lesson 87

Lesson Focus: Jesus continues to heal many

Opening prayer...

Bible Verse

Matthew 15:30 (NKJV) "Then great multitudes came to Him, having with them the lame, blind, mute, maimed, and many others; and they laid them down at Jesus' feet, and He healed them."

What do you already know?

What do you want to know?

Bible Lesson

Jesus and His disciples were in an area known as Tyre of Sidon, and Jesus entered into a house but did not want anyone to know that He was there. Jesus was so well known, though; he could not be hidden. A Canaanite woman came before them and cried out to Jesus, "Son of David, have mercy, my daughter has many demons." Jesus did not say anything to her, and the disciples asked Jesus if He could send her away because she kept crying out to them. Jesus still remained quiet about the woman. Jesus finally answered and said, "I am only called to the lost sheep of Israel." She continued to cry out to Jesus, "Please help me!" Jesus said to her, "It is not good to take the children's bread and throw it to the little dogs." Jesus said this because He was called to the lost sheep of Israel. She was one of the others that needed help. She answered Jesus, "Even little dogs eat the crumbs that fall from their master's table." She told Jesus that even though she was not one of the chosen sheep He was called to, He could still heal her daughter if He wanted. Jesus said that the woman had great faith, and Jesus healed the woman's daughter at that very moment.

Something new that I learned today was:

Matthew 15:30 (NKJV) "Then great multitudes came to Him, having with them the lame, blind, mute, maimed, and many others; and they laid them down at Jesus' feet, and He healed them."

Write and Draw Box

Unit 3: Lesson 88

Lesson Focus: Jesus continues to heal many

Opening prayer...

Bible Verse

Matthew 15:30 (NKJV) "Then great multitudes came to Him, having with them the lame, blind, mute, maimed, and many others; and they laid them down at Jesus' feet, and He healed them."

What do you already know?

What do you want to know?

Bible Lesson

The disciples and Jesus went out from that region, and they were near the Sea of Galilee, and the people brought to Him a man who was deaf and could not talk correctly. The people begged Jesus to put His hand on him, and Jesus took the man aside from the great numbers of people. Jesus put His fingers in the man's ears; he spit and touched the man's tongue. Jesus then looked up to heaven and sighed, and He said, "Be opened!" The man's ears opened instantly, and his tongue was loosed from that moment on. Jesus commanded the people that they should not tell anyone about what had happened. Still, the more that Jesus commanded them not to say anything, the more they told others about what Jesus was doing. All of the people were so amazed that Jesus could do these things. Many knew that Jesus was from the area, and they knew His family. "What man could do these things," they thought to themselves. They did not know that He was conceived by the Holy Spirit inside His mother, Mary. Jesus did have an earthly father, but He also had a heavenly Father. Jesus is God's Son who came to us in the form of a human. He was God in the flesh, as the Bible says. Jesus still performs miracles, signs, and wonders today. Believe in your heart that He can heal you and those around you, and He will begin to use you to pray for others, and they will be healed in the name of Jesus.

Something new that I learned today was:

Matthew 15:30 (NKJV) **"Then great multitudes came to Him, having with them the lame, blind, mute, maimed, and many others; and they laid them down at Jesus' feet, and He healed them."**

Write and Draw Box

Unit 3 Week 22: Assessment

Lesson Focus: Jesus calms the storm

Opening prayer...

Bible Verse: Write or tell the Bible verse to your parent.

Luke 8:24b (NKJV) "Then He arose and rebuked the _____ and the raging of the water. And they ceased, and there was a _____."

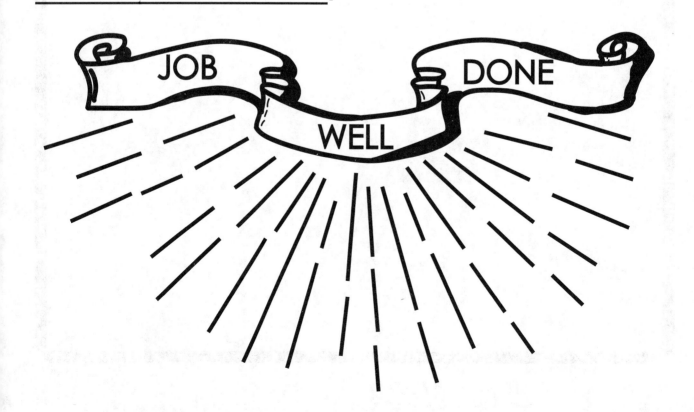

Write, draw or tell your parents what you learned this week. Talk about your favorite things.

Unit 3: Lesson 89

Lesson Focus: Jesus feeds thousands of people

Opening prayer...

Bible Verse
Matthew 14:16 (NKJV)
"But Jesus said to them, "They do not need to go away. You give them something to eat."

What do you already know?

What do you want to know?

Bible Lesson

Jesus heard the news that His cousin John had been killed in prison, and He sailed away by boat to a quiet place to be by Himself. Many people heard that Jesus would be in their area, so they went out to see Him. When Jesus landed on the shore, the people saw Him, and He had compassion on them because they were like sheep without a shepherd. He began to teach them, and healed all of the sick people there. It was about evening time now, and the people did not have any food to eat. The disciples told Jesus to send the people away because it was getting dark. They needed to go into the villages and get something to eat. Jesus said that they did not need to send the people away, and they should feed the people themselves. The disciples told Jesus that it would take about a year's wages to feed all of the people there. They asked Jesus, "Should we go out and spend that much money on food for these people?" Jesus said to the disciples, "Go and see how much food that the people have." The disciples gathered all the food from the people they could, and they came up with five loaves of bread and two fish. Jesus told the people to sit together in groups on the grass. The people sat together in groups of fifty and one hundred. Jesus took the food in His hands, looked up to heaven towards His Father, and gave Him thanks for the food. He gave the food back to the disciples and told them to pass it out to the people. They passed out the food, miraculously multiplied by God, and all of the people were fed. There were even twelve baskets full left over. They all ate and were satisfied, and about five thousand men had eaten that day, not including the women and children there. Jesus still cares about you today. He will not ever let you go hungry because He will provide for you. He is the same yesterday, today, and forever.

Something new that I learned today was:

Matthew 14:16 (NKJV) "But Jesus said to them, "They do not need to go away. You give them something to eat."

Write and Draw Box

Unit 3: Lesson 90

Lesson Focus: Jesus feeds thousands of people

Opening prayer...

Bible Verse
Matthew 14:16 (NKJV)
"But Jesus said to them, "They do not need to go away. You give them something to eat."

What do you already know?

What do you want to know?

Bible Lesson

Jesus and His disciples were near the Sea of Galilee, and a large crowd of people had gathered around them to hear Jesus teach. Jesus also healed many who were sick. Jesus asked His disciples to come over to Him. He told them that He had compassion on the people because they had been with Him for three days now, and they had not eaten. Jesus said, "If I send them away now without any food, they will fall over on their way home because many have come from a long distance." The disciples said to Jesus, "We are in a remote place, and there is no place to get food for all of these people." Jesus asked them how much food that they had. They said that they had seven loaves of bread. Jesus took the bread and lifted it up to heaven, gave thanks for it to His Father, and He gave it back to the disciples to give to the people. They passed out the food to all of the people, and God had multiplied food again. They had seven baskets full of bread left over after passing out the bread to the people. After all of the people ate, Jesus sent the people away so that they could go back to their hometowns. About four thousand people ate the multiplied food that day. After the people went away, Jesus and the disciples got into a boat to head to another area. We can learn so much from this story today. Jesus has compassion for people, and He does not want to see people hurt in any way. He will provide for us when we need things. Just ask Him for His will to be done here on earth as it is in heaven. Never forget, He loves you, and you are valuable to Him.

Something new that I learned today was:

Matthew 14:16 (NKJV) "But Jesus said to them, "They do not need to go away. You give them something to eat."

Write and Draw Box

Unit 3: Lesson 91

Lesson Focus: The <u>Transfiguration</u>

Opening prayer...

Bible Verse
Matthew 17:2 (NKJV)
"There he was transfigured before them. His face shone like the sun, and his clothes became as white as the light."

What do you already know?

What do you want to know?

Bible Lesson

Jesus began to tell His disciples that He must go to Jerusalem to suffer, die, and then be raised back to life again on the third day. Peter took Jesus aside and began to tell Him that these things would not happen. Jesus rebuked Peter and said to him, "Get behind me satan, for you do not have in mind the things of God." Peter wanted to see Jesus set up as an earthly king, and Peter was willing to fight to protect Jesus. This is why he later cut off the ear of the high priest's servant when they came to get Jesus and arrest Him. Peter carried a sword around to protect Jesus. Remember, many people often surrounded Jesus, and many wanted to kill Jesus. After about six to eight days, Jesus took Peter, James, and John with Him to go up to a high mountain by themselves to pray. Jesus must have often had a tough time getting alone because so many people wanted to be healed and ministered to by Him. As Jesus was praying to His Father, His face became as bright as the sun, and His clothes were as white as lightning. Moses and Elijah appeared in their heavenly glory before Jesus and started talking with Him just as this happened. The Bible says that they all spoke about spoke about Jesus leaving the earth and when it would happen. Jesus would do this by going to Jerusalem and suffering many things at the hands of the religious leaders.

Something new that I learned today was:

Matthew 17:2 (NKJV) "There he was transfigured before them. His face shone like the sun, and his clothes became as white as the light."

Write and Draw Box

Unit 3: Lesson 92

Lesson Focus: The Transfiguration

Opening prayer...

Bible Verse
Matthew 17:2 (NKJV)

"There he was transfigured before them. His face shone like the sun, and his clothes became as white as the light."

What do you already know?

What do you want to know?

Bible Lesson

While Jesus, Moses, and Elijah were all talking about when Jesus would soon suffer in Jerusalem at the hands of the religious leaders, Peter, James, and John were very sleepy. They saw Jesus, Moses, and Elijah standing there in their heavenly glory when they woke up fully. Peter said to Jesus, "We should build three shelters here because of what has happened, one for you, one for Moses, and one for Elijah." Peter did not really know what he was saying. While they were speaking, a bright, thick cloud covered them, and a voice spoke from the cloud. The voice said, "This is my Son who I have chosen and with whom I am well pleased. Listen to Him." This voice was God the Father speaking to the disciples, telling them to listen to Jesus. After the disciples heard this voice, they were very scared and put their faces to the ground. Jesus came over to them and told them not to be afraid and to get up. When they all got up, it was just Jesus standing there before them. Moses, Elijah, and God the Father who spoke from within the cloud had gone back to where they came from. After all of these things happened, they were all going down the mountain, and Jesus told them that they were not to tell anyone what had happened upon the mountain until after he had risen from the dead. The disciples kept all that they had witnessed to themselves until after the resurrection of Jesus.

Something new that I learned today was:

Matthew 17:2 (NKJV) "There he was transfigured before them. His face shone like the sun, and his clothes became as white as the light."

Write and Draw Box

Unit 3 Week 23: Assessment

Lesson Focus: Jesus feeds thousands of people

Opening prayer...

Bible Verse: Write or tell the Bible verse to your parent.

Matthew 14:16 (NKJV)

"But _____ said to them,

"They do not need to go away. You give them

something to _____."

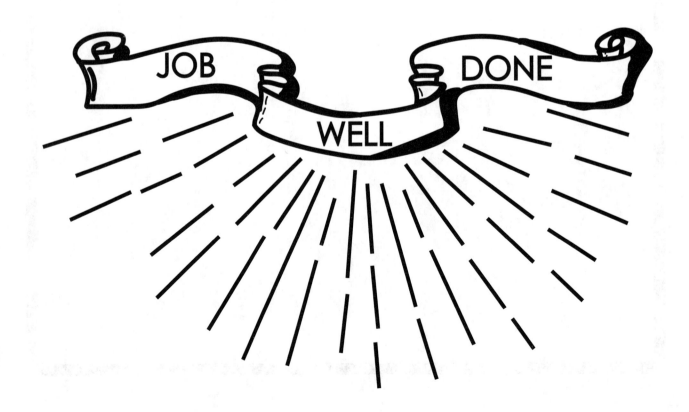

Write, draw or tell your parents what you learned this week. Talk about your favorite things.

Unit 3: Lesson 93

Lesson Focus: Jesus loves little children

Opening prayer...

Bible Verse
Matthew 19:14 (NKJV)
"But Jesus said, "Let the little children come to Me, and do not forbid them; for of such is the kingdom of heaven."

What do you already know?

What do you want to know?

Bible Lesson

Many children and infants were brought before Jesus so that He could bless them. Jesus would pray for the children and bless them as they came to Him. Jesus' disciples rebuked the children for going to Jesus. Jesus saw that His disciples were rebuking the little children so they would not come to Him. He told the disciples, "Do not forbid the little children from coming to Me, for such is the kingdom of God." Jesus went on to say to all who were listening, "Whoever does not receive the kingdom of God as a little child will by no means enter it." (Mark 10:15 NKJV) Jesus gives us a great lesson here that we should pay attention to. When a person accepts Jesus as their Savior and begins to grow as a Christian, that person must come to the Lord as a little child would. We must have an open heart that has nothing in the way. Children have no hindrances and no prior beliefs or unbeliefs that can hinder their growth. Jesus took the children up into His arms and continued to bless them. Jesus loves children. He wants to bless you today. Jesus tells us that you must come to the kingdom as a little child would. Let nothing hold you back from serving Him with all of your heart. Do not let anyone tell you that you cannot do something for God. You can do all things through Jesus Christ, who strengthens you. Pour out your heart to Him today, and He will continue to use you for His glory. He loves you so much, and He has a great plan for you.

Something new that I learned today was:

Matthew 19:14 (NKJV) "But Jesus said, "Let the little children come to Me, and do not forbid them; for of such is the kingdom of heaven."

Write and Draw Box

Unit 3: Lesson 94

Lesson Focus: Jesus loves little children

Opening prayer...

Bible Verse
Matthew 19:14 (NKJV)
"But Jesus said, "Let the little children come to Me, and do not forbid them; for of such is the kingdom of heaven."

What do you already know?

What do you want to know?

Bible Lesson

Jesus loves children very much, and He desires for you to seek Him each and every day. Do not let anyone look down on you because you are young. God will use you, and it does not matter what your age is. Here are some more Bible verses about children found throughout the Bible: "Behold, children are a heritage from the LORD, the fruit of the womb is a reward." (Ps.127:3 NKJV) "My frame was not hidden from you when I was made in secret, and skillfully wrought in the lowest parts of the earth." 16 "Your eyes saw my substance, being yet unformed. And in Your book they all were written, the days fashioned for me when as yet there were none of them." (Ps.139:15-16 NKJV) "Train up a child in the way he should go, and when he is old, he will not depart from it." (Prov. 22:6 NKJV) "Take heed that you do not despise one of these little ones, for I say to you that in heaven their angels always see the face of My Father who is in heaven." (Matt.18:10 NKJV) As you can see, throughout the Bible, many different scriptures talk about children. Even before you were formed in your mother, He was there, and He wrote a book about you and your life. This is why we pray "Your will be done on earth as it is in heaven," when we pray. We agree with what He has written down for us each and every day. Seek after what His will is for your life today. Ask Him to speak to you, and He will. He loves you, and He cannot wait to spend time with you. You are valued by Him.

Something new that I learned today was:

Matthew 19:14 (NKJV) "But Jesus said, "Let the little children come to Me, and do not forbid them; for of such is the kingdom of heaven."

Write and Draw Box

Unit 3: Lesson 95

Lesson Focus: Zacchaeus

Opening prayer...

Bible Verse
Luke 19:10 (NKJV)

"For the Son of Man has come to seek and to save that which was lost."

What do you already know?

What do you want to know?

Bible Lesson

Jesus was traveling when He came to a city named Jericho. He was just going to pass through the city of Jericho. A wealthy man named Zacchaeus lived there, and he was a chief tax collector. During this time period in history, many people did not like tax collectors because they took people's money. Tax collectors were just supposed to collect the people's taxes. Still, many times the tax collectors would collect extra money for themselves. Because of this, tax collectors were associated with sinners. Jesus was very popular throughout all of Israel, and many crowds followed Jesus wherever He went. When Jesus entered Jericho, many people surrounded Him, and Zacchaeus was one of the people that wanted to see Jesus. Zacchaeus was a short man, and because the crowds of people were so great surrounding Jesus, Zacchaeus could not see Him. Zacchaeus decided to climb up a sycamore-fig tree to try to see Jesus when He passed by. Finally, Jesus reached the area where Zacchaeus was waiting. As the crowds of people pushed around Jesus, hoping to just touch Him and be healed, Jesus looked over and saw Zacchaeus up in the tree. Jesus called out to Zacchaeus and told him to come out of the tree immediately. Jesus said to Zacchaeus, "I must stay at your house today." Jesus cares about everyone. He saw a tax collector, a man who was usually known as a sinner, and He said to him, "I must stay at your house today."

Something new that I learned today was:

Luke 19:10 (NKJV) "For the Son of Man has come to seek and to save that which was lost."

Write and Draw Box

Unit 3: Lesson 96

Lesson Focus: Zacchaeus

Opening prayer...

Bible Verse
Luke 19:10 (NKJV)

"For the Son of Man has come to seek and to save that which was lost."

What do you already know?

What do you want to know?

Bible Lesson

Jesus saw Zacchaeus up in the fig tree and told him that He must stay at his house. Zacchaeus came down out of the tree and welcomed Jesus into his home. Zacchaeus was happy that Jesus had talked to him and that this famous man was going to stay at his home. Zacchaeus was a rich man, and he probably had other wealthy friends. Many times, in society, wealthy people like to compete to see who knows the most popular people. It was good for Zacchaeus to welcome Jesus into his home because Jesus was a very popular man. The people from the city began to see that Jesus was going to stay at Zacchaeus' house. They said to themselves, "Why is Jesus going to dine with this sinner ?" I believe that Zacchaeus heard what the people were saying about him. He said out loud to Jesus and everyone who was there, "Right now, I give half of everything that I own to the poor. If I have cheated anyone in the past out of any money, I will pay them back four times the amount." I am not sure if Zacchaeus did this just to be noticed by everyone and to look good in front of Jesus or not. Jesus did say to Zacchaeus after he had said these things, "Today, salvation has come to this house because this man is also a son of Abraham." Jesus went on to say, "I have come to seek and save that which was lost." Jesus was talking about sinners. Jesus also says in another scripture, "It is not the healthy who need a doctor, but the sick." Jesus did not come for the righteous, but He came for the sinners. If we can truly understand this today, it will change our lives. We must go and do what Jesus did. We must seek out the lost, the sinners, just as Jesus did and tell them about the good news of the gospel.

Something new that I learned today was:

Luke 19:10 (NKJV) "For the Son of Man has come to seek and to save that which was lost."

Write and Draw Box

Unit 3 Week 24: Assessment

Lesson Focus: Jesus loves little children/Zacchaeus

Opening prayer...

Bible Verse: Write or tell the Bible verse to your parent.

Luke 19:10 (NKJV)

"For the _____ of Man has

come to seek and to _____ that

which was lost."

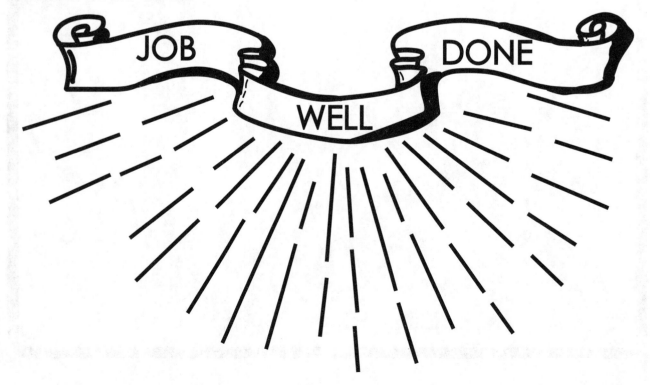

Write, draw or tell your parents what you learned this week. Talk about your favorite things.

Unit 3: Lesson 97

Lesson Focus: The good Samaritan

Opening prayer...

Bible Verse
Luke 10:25 (NKJV)

"And behold, a certain lawyer stood up and tested Him, saying, "Teacher, what shall I do to inherit eternal life?"

What do you already know?

What do you want to know?

Bible Lesson

Jesus often taught in the temple area and in many other regions. One of these times that Jesus was teaching, a lawyer stood up and asked Jesus a question. The lawyer asked Jesus, "What must I do to inherit eternal life?" Jesus asked the man, "What is written in the Law about it, and what have you read about this?" The man answered Jesus, " 'You shall love the LORD your God with all your heart, with all your soul, with all your strength, and with all your mind,' and 'love your neighbor as yourself.' " (Luke 10:27 NKJV) Jesus replied, "You have answered correctly. If you do this, you will live." After Jesus said these things, the man wanted to justify himself, and he said to Jesus, "Who is my neighbor?" Jesus answered the man by telling a parable. A parable is a story that teaches a spiritual lesson using a real-life situation. This is why when Jesus told parables, he used fishing, farming, and other things that were the jobs and things that people often did in that time in history. This parable that Jesus began telling the man is often called the good Samaritan. Again, a parable relates to people and their daily lives, and here Jesus was talking about Samaritans, who were not liked by the Jewish people. Jesus related to the people of the day, and He still understands and knows us today. Jesus went around doing good, and He loved people. He loves you also, and He values you.

Something new that I learned today was:

Luke 10:25 (NKJV) "And behold, a certain lawyer stood up and tested Him, saying, "Teacher, what shall I do to inherit eternal life?"

Write and Draw Box

Unit 3: Lesson 98

Lesson Focus: The good Samaritan

Opening prayer...

Bible Verse
Luke 10:25 (NKJV)
"And behold, a certain lawyer stood up and tested Him, saying, "Teacher, what shall I do to inherit eternal life?"

What do you already know?

What do you want to know?

Bible Lesson

Jesus began telling a story called a parable to the crowd. The parable is: A man was traveling from Jerusalem to Jericho, and along the way, he was robbed by some thieves. The thieves took the man's clothing and beat him, almost killing him. The thieves left the man and thought that he was dead. A priest was walking by and saw the half-dead man on the side of the road. He went to the other side of the road to avoid the man. A Levite man also passed by the same way as the priest and did not stop to help the man. But, a Samaritan man came walking down the road, and when he saw the beaten man, he had compassion on him. He helped bandage the man's wounds and put some healing oils on him. The Samaritan man put the injured man on his animal to carry him to an inn. The Samaritan man made sure that the injured man was taken care of at the inn, and he said to the innkeeper, "Please take care of the man, and I will pay you whatever it takes." The man gave the innkeeper some money and said he would pay the innkeeper back for any extra costs needed to help the injured man. After He was done telling this story, Jesus asked those who were listening, "Who then is a neighbor to the man who was injured and beaten?" The people answered Jesus, "The man who had mercy on the injured man and helped him." Jesus said to the people listening, "Go and do the same to others." Today, we can learn an important lesson from this parable. Jesus cares about all people, and He loves you very much. He expects us to love other people just as He has loved us. As you go about your day today, remember to treat others with kindness and love others as you want to be loved.

Something new that I learned today was:

Luke 10:25 (NKJV) "And behold, a certain lawyer stood up and tested Him, saying, "Teacher, what shall I do to inherit eternal life?"

Write and Draw Box

Unit 3: Lesson 99

Lesson Focus: The prodigal son

Opening prayer...

Bible Verse
Luke 15:24 (NKJV)

**"For this my son was dead and is alive again; he was lost and is found.'
And they began to be merry."**

What do you already know?

What do you want to know?

Bible Lesson

A man had two sons, and the younger son asked his father if he could have a part of his <u>inheritance</u> early. So, the father divided up his things between the two boys. After a few days, the younger brother gathered all his belongings and left his father's home. He journeyed to a faraway country where he quickly spent all of his inheritance because he was living very wastefully. This type of living is called prodigal living. A prodigal is someone who wastes their money on things, and they are not careful with their spending. After he had spent everything that he had, there was a great famine in the land. He became in great need of basic things like food, clothing, and such. The son went to a person that lived in that land and asked them for a job. The person from that country allowed the son to feed his pigs. The son often became so hungry that he thought about eating the food that he gave to the pigs. No one gave him any food and supplies, and he was very hungry. The son realized that he was not going to make it if he continued to live like he was. He realized that even his father's servants were treated better than he was right now, and they even ate better than he was eating right now. He thought to himself, "Maybe if I go to my father and tell him that I am no longer worthy of being called his son, he would possibly hire me as one of his servants. At least I would have something to eat." We can learn many things from this story. One thing that we can remember is that we should honor our parents and those who are older. These people have a lot of wisdom and years of experience living life, and we can learn from their mistakes.

Something new that I learned today was:

Luke 15:24 (NKJV) "For this my son was dead and is alive again; he was lost and is found.' And they began to be merry."

Write and Draw Box

Unit 3: Lesson 100

Lesson Focus: The prodigal son

Opening prayer...

Bible Verse
Luke 15:24 (NKJV)
"For this my son was dead and is alive again; he was lost and is found.' And they began to be merry."

What do you already know?

What do you want to know?

Bible Lesson

The youngest son had spent all of his inheritance. He was about to eat the pigs' food when he realized that even the servants at his father's house ate better than him. He decided to get up and go back to his father's house to see if he would accept him as one of his servants. He headed back home and when his father saw him coming in the distance, he had compassion for his son, and he ran to him and kissed him. The father told his servants to bring a ring, put it on his hand, and get him some sandals to wear. The father told them that they should bring the fatted calf and kill it so they could have a feast, and so they could eat and be happy. "For this, my son was dead and is alive again; he was lost and is found." (Luke 15:24 NKJV) The older son was in the field working when he heard all of the laughter and noise from the people celebrating. He asked the servants what was happening, and they told him that his youngest brother had come home. The older brother was angry, and his father pleaded with him to celebrate. The oldest son said to his father, "I have been working and serving you for all these years, and you have not even given me a goat to eat with my friends to be happy." The father said to him, "You have always been with me, and everything I have is yours, and you should be happy now and rejoice because your brother who was once dead is now alive again. He was lost, and now he is found." This story is a great story of forgiveness and acceptance by the father. We also have forgiveness and acceptance from our heavenly Father. We can always come home. We can do nothing where He will not accept us back with loving arms of acceptance. Your Father loves you so much, and you are accepted.

Something new that I learned today was:

Luke 15:24 (NKJV) "For this my son was dead and is alive again; he was lost and is found.' And they began to be merry."

Write and Draw Box

Unit 3 Week 25: Assessment

Lesson Focus: The good Samaritan/The prodigal son

Opening prayer...

Bible Verse: Write or tell the Bible verse to your parent.

Luke 15:24 (NKJV)

"For this my _____ was dead and is alive again; he was lost and is _____.' And they began to be merry."

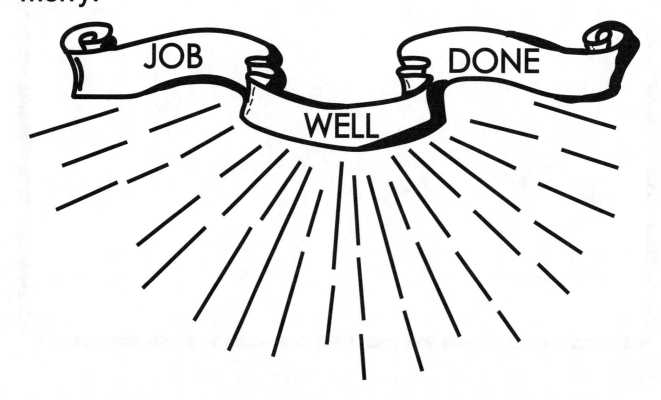

Write, draw or tell your parents what you learned this week. Talk about your favorite things.

Unit 3: Lesson 101

Lesson Focus: Paul the apostle

Opening prayer...

Bible Verse
Acts 9:4 (NKJV)
"Then he fell to the ground, and heard a voice saying to him, "Saul, Saul, why are you persecuting Me?"

What do you already know?

What do you want to know?

Bible Lesson

A man named Saul was highly trained in Judaism, even more than many others his own age. Saul was a Pharisee, and he was very zealous for the traditions of his fathers. He would do anything to <u>preserve</u> their traditions. Saul knew the Law and followed its teachings very closely. Because of this, when Saul heard that a new group of people followed after the teachings of Jesus of Nazareth, he <u>persecuted</u> these Christians. Saul was even a witness, giving his consent, when some early followers were killed for their faith. Saul and other Pharisees like him went into the homes of people who were thought to be Christians, and they dragged them out of their houses and sent them to prison. Because of the great persecution that the new Christians faced, many scattered out across the region. Wherever the persecuted Christians went, they still preached the good news of Jesus Christ. The Bible also says in Acts 9 that Saul was threatening the disciples of the Lord. He went to the high priest and asked for letters that would give him the authority to bind any followers of Christ and take them to Jerusalem. This same passage calls the early Christians who followed Christ those who were a part of the Way. This is most likely because when Jesus taught, He said that He was the Way, the Truth, and the Life, and no one comes to the Father but through Him.

Something new that I learned today was:

Acts 9:4 (NKJV) "Then he fell to the ground, and heard a voice saying to him, "Saul, Saul, why are you persecuting Me?"

Write and Draw Box

Unit 3: Lesson 102

Lesson Focus: Paul the apostle

Opening prayer...

Bible Verse
Acts 9:4 (NKJV)
"Then he fell to the ground, and heard a voice saying to him, "Saul, Saul, why are you persecuting Me?"

What do you already know?

What do you want to know?

Bible Lesson

Saul was still persecuting the Christians who followed the Way. He was on the road to the city of Damascus, and a bright light came down upon him from heaven. He fell down to the ground, and a voice came from the light saying to him, "Saul, Saul, why are you persecuting Me?" Saul wondered who was talking to him, so he asked, "Who are you?" The voice said, "I am Jesus, who you are persecuting." Jesus told Saul that it would be hard for him to stand against the Lord and that fighting him was a losing battle. Saul responded to Jesus and said, "What do you want me to do?" Jesus replied and said to Saul, "Go to the city and do what I tell you to do." There were people there with them, and they also heard the voice, but did not see the bright light. Saul got up from the ground, and he was blinded by the bright light, so those with him had to lead him to the next city. For the next three days, Saul did not have any sight, and he did not eat and drink during that time. When he arrived in Damascus, there was a man named Ananias, who the Lord had spoken to about Saul. The Lord told Ananias that Saul would be used to proclaim His name before kings, Gentiles, and the children of Israel. Ananias went to Saul and told him that the Lord sent him to Saul so that he could receive his sight back. Ananias prayed for Saul, and something like scales fell from Saul's eyes. A while later, Saul became known as Paul, who would write many of the New Testament books of the Bible.

Something new that I learned today was:

Acts 9:4 (NKJV) "Then he fell to the ground, and heard a voice saying to him, "Saul, Saul, why are you persecuting Me?"

Write and Draw Box

Unit 3: Lesson 103

Lesson Focus: Paul talks to the Romans

Opening prayer...

Bible Verse
Romans 1:8 (NKJV)
"First, I thank my God through Jesus Christ for you all, that your faith is spoken of throughout the whole world."

What do you already know?

What do you want to know?

Bible Lesson

The Apostle Paul wrote many of the New Testament books. Most of the books that he wrote were letters to different communities or cities. A few of his other books were written to specific people or people groups like the Hebrews. Paul's letter to the Roman Christians points out that he would like to visit Rome in the future, but he has been hindered. Paul tells the Romans that he is ready to preach the gospel of Jesus Christ to them. He also addresses the wickedness that he has heard that the people were doing there in Rome and explains that it will not be good for those people during the judgment of God. Paul goes on to praise those who have been doing good in the sight of the Lord. Paul also lets the people of Rome know that God does not have favorites. He tells them that all have sinned, both Jews and Greeks. Everyone who has ever lived has sinned, except Jesus Christ, who lived a sinless life while here on the earth. This is the reason why we need a Savior. It is only through the blood of Jesus that we can have forgiveness of sins. Paul talks about this a lot to the Romans. The letter highlights the forgiveness of sins, and that God demonstrated His love to us by sending Jesus Christ His Son while we were sinners. This means that we come to Jesus as we are, and we do not have to clean ourselves up first. Jesus helps us live a <u>righteous</u> life by teaching us to live holy, as we read the Word of God and pray.

Something new that I learned today was:

Romans 1:8 (NKJV) " First, I thank my God through Jesus Christ for you all, that your faith is spoken of throughout the whole world."

Write and Draw Box

Unit 3: Lesson 104

Lesson Focus: Paul talks to the Romans

Opening prayer...

Bible Verse
Romans 1:8 (NKJV)
"First, I thank my God through Jesus Christ for you all, that your faith is spoken of throughout the whole world."

What do you already know?

What do you want to know?

Bible Lesson

When Paul wrote to the Romans, he talked about Adam, who was the first man to sin and bring sin into the world. Just like Adam was the first man, Jesus was a new beginning for mankind. Only through Jesus Christ can we find forgiveness for sins. When we accept Him into our hearts and lives, He washes us new, and we are blameless before Him like Adam was before he sinned. As Christians, we are dead to sin now and are alive in Christ. We are no longer slaves to sin; we are slaves to righteousness. We do not let sin reign in our body; we are set free from sin. The Bible says, that if we are led by the Spirit of God, then we are sons of God. We are joint-heirs with Jesus Christ, God is our Father, so we are His heirs. An heir has all of the rights and privileges from the Father, and whatever He has, it is ours because we are rightful heirs. Paul wrote about Israel rejecting Jesus as Messiah and that they should have seen that Jesus was the fulfillment of the prophecies in the Old Testament. Paul would not give up on the people of Israel, and we should not either. Today, the Israelite people are still looking for the Messiah. We need to share with them that Jesus Christ is the promised Messiah that already came for us. Paul tells the Romans that they must live like they are Christians and flee from the things of the world. Just like Paul says, we too must flee from evil and do good. We must overcome evil with good.

Something new that I learned today was:

Romans 1:8 (NKJV) " First, I thank my God through Jesus Christ for you all, that your faith is spoken of throughout the whole world."

Write and Draw Box

Unit 3 Week 26: Assessment

Lesson Focus: Paul the Apostle

Opening prayer...

Bible Verse: Write or tell the Bible verse to your parent.

Romans 1:8 (NKJV) " First, I thank my God through

_____ for you all, that your

faith is _____ of throughout

the whole world."

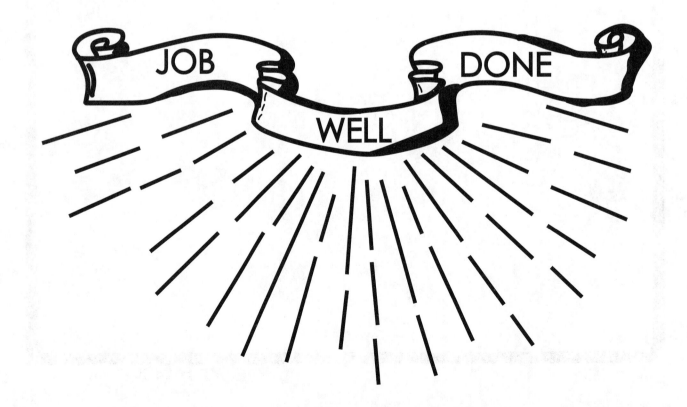

Write, draw or tell your parents what you learned this week. Talk about your favorite things.

Unit 3: Lesson 105

Lesson Focus: Paul talks to the Corinthians

Opening prayer...

Bible Verse
I Corinthians 1:9 (NKJV)
"God is faithful, by whom you were called into the fellowship of His Son, Jesus Christ our Lord."

What do you already know?

What do you want to know?

Bible Lesson

Paul started off his letter to the Corinthians and most of his letters by greeting the Christians and encouraging them in the Lord. After his encouragement, he then often addressed some issues that had arisen in the area. In Corinth, there had been some who held men higher than the Lord. Paul told them, "Did I die for you like Christ did? Were you baptized in the name of Paul?" No, they were not, and this problem even exists today in many churches. People tend to lift up a man instead of lifting up Christ, who died for us. We must not look to man for salvation and healing; we look to God. The Lord uses men and women to bring these lessons to people, but only through the Lord can we be saved and healed. Paul wrote to the Corinthians about God choosing the weak things of the world to put to shame the things that are mighty. Jesus chose fishermen, tax collectors, and a former persecutor of Christians to be the early church leaders. The Lord still does this today. He can and will use anyone, especially those who the world thinks cannot complete the task. Paul tells the Christians there that they need to grow up and mature in the faith. Paul said that he had been feeding them the milk of the word, the basic things, and that they were still not ready for the meat of the word, the deeper things of God. There is an important lesson here to learn. We must continually grow in Christ. We must read God's Word and talk to Him each day. The more time that we spend with Him, the greater that we will know Him. This is the most important lesson for you to learn. Spend time with Jesus. He loves you, and He has a plan for your life. Talk to Him today, and listen to what He is saying to you and obey. You are valued by Him.

Something new that I learned today was:

I Corinthians 1:9 (NKJV) " God is faithful, by whom you were called into the fellowship of His Son, Jesus Christ our Lord."

Write and Draw Box

Unit 3: Lesson 106

Lesson Focus: Paul talks to the Corinthians

Opening prayer...

Bible Verse
I Corinthians 1:9 (NKJV)
"God is faithful, by whom you were called into the fellowship of His Son, Jesus Christ our Lord."

What do you already know?

What do you want to know?

Bible Lesson

Paul tells the Corinthians that the wisdom of this world is foolishness. Paul was very well trained, and Corinth was well known for its great philosophers. These people spoke about things in the marketplaces and theaters for all to hear their great wisdom. So, Paul tells them not to be wise in their own eyes because who can really boast about their own knowledge? Does not all wisdom come from above? Paul says that we have become wise in Christ. He tells them that he has been beaten, shipwrecked, in prison, without food, and he continues to tell them about his hardships. He gave them an example that if they follow after Christ and His teachings, they too may face these things. They must count it all joy if they were to suffer for the name of Jesus because they would be rewarded in eternity. Paul tells them some of the things that he has heard that they have been doing that are wrong and sinful and tells them that they must repent. Paul encourages them and tells them that they were bought with a price, that they are to glorify God with their bodies, and not to give in to their sinful desires. Jesus paid a great price for us all. He died for us while we were yet sinners. The Bible says that we can come to Him, ask Him for forgiveness, turn away from our sins, and He will cleanse us from all unrighteousness. Paul uses a great example of a person running a race, explains that a runner who runs a race always runs to win. We must also think this way about our lives. We live our days with Christ knowing that He has already won the race we call life for us. We must run in such a way that we will win the prize. The prize that awaits us is our crown in heaven. We will receive a crown for what we have done for Him while here on earth. It is all about our obedience to Him. Pray today, "Your will be done on earth as it is in heaven in my life Lord."

Something new that I learned today was:

I Corinthians 1:9 (NKJV) " God is faithful, by whom you were called into the fellowship of His Son, Jesus Christ our Lord."

Write and Draw Box

Unit 3: Lesson 107

Lesson Focus: Paul talks to the Galatians

Opening prayer...

Bible Verse
Galatians 1:23 (NKJV)
"But they were hearing only, "He who formerly persecuted us now preaches the faith which he once tried to destroy."

What do you already know?

What do you want to know?

Bible Lesson

Paul greets the church in Galatia and then starts addressing the issues he has heard about in Galatia. Paul says that the people have been turning away from the gospel of Jesus Christ and following after a different gospel. Paul says that the gospel he preaches is not from man. It is from his revelation from Jesus Christ. He shares with the Galatians that those who have been listening to his message have been spying on him to try to bring bondage to him and the gospel, because they saw the freedom that Paul and the followers of Christ had. Paul talks about being trained in Judaism, and how he followed the Law very closely because he was well trained. He even states that there were not many who were more trained in Judaism than him, and he was very zealous for the things of the law. Paul goes on to talk about when Peter, one of the disciples, came to Paul, and he was eating meat and all the things that those who follow the beliefs of Judaism do not eat. Paul rebuked Peter and asked him why he had been eating what the Gentile foods, because Paul had training in Judaism which forbids eating certain foods. Paul then continues on to tell them that in Christ, there is no Jew or Greek, and we are all one in Jesus Christ. We are all brothers and sisters in Christ, and we are children and heirs of Christ.

Something new that I learned today was:

Galatians 1:23 (NKJV) "But they were hearing only, "He who formerly persecuted us now preaches the faith which he once tried to destroy."

Write and Draw Box

Unit 3: Lesson 108

Lesson Focus: Paul talks to the Galatians

Opening prayer...

Bible Verse
Galatians 1:23 (NKJV)
"But they were hearing only, "He who formerly persecuted us now preaches the faith which he once tried to destroy."

What do you already know?

What do you want to know?

Bible Lesson

Paul continues to tell the Galatians that they must help one another with their burdens. If someone needs to be restored to the faith, it must be done gently. Each person must examine themselves and not be deceived. Whatever a man gives out to others, he shall also have that coming back to him. If you are always angry towards others, you will get anger back from others. If you do not help others, then others probably will not want to help you. A person who sows into the flesh, which means giving into your fleshly desires, will reap the flesh. Those who sow into the Spirit will reap the Spirit and everlasting life. We should always do good to others, especially to those who are believers in Jesus Christ. Paul tells the Galatians that he has taught them what to do, and now they must not trouble him about these things anymore. Paul tells them that he bears on his body the marks of Christ. He shares with them that he had been beaten just as Jesus Christ was beaten for us. He tells them not to walk in the flesh, but to walk in the Spirit. To walk in the Spirit, we must have the fruits of the Spirit within us. The fruits of the Spirit are love, joy, peace, patience, kindness, goodness, faithfulness, gentleness, and self-control. If we live in the Spirit, we will also walk in the Spirit. We must follow these teachings from the apostle Paul to walk through each day living in the Spirit.

Something new that I learned today was:

Galatians 1:23 (NKJV) "But they were hearing only, "He who formerly persecuted us now preaches the faith which he once tried to destroy."

Write and Draw Box

Unit 3 Week 27: Assessment

Lesson Focus: Corinthians / Galatians

Opening prayer...

Bible Verse: Write or tell the Bible verse to your parent.

Galatians 1:23 (NKJV) "But they were

_____ only, "He who formerly

persecuted us now _____ the

faith which he once tried to destroy."

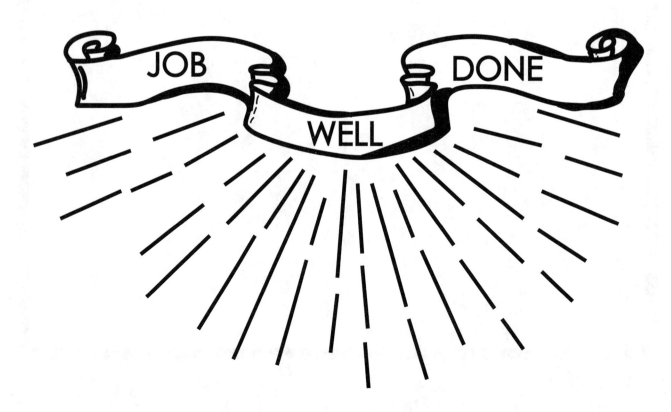

Write, draw or tell your parents what you learned this week. Talk about your favorite things.

Unit 3: Lesson 109

Lesson Focus: Paul talks to the Ephesians

Opening prayer...

Bible Verse

Ephesians 1:18 (NKJV) " The eyes of your understanding being enlightened; that you may know what is the hope of His calling, what are the riches of the glory of His inheritance in the saints."

What do you already know?

What do you want to know?

Bible Lesson

Paul starts off his letter to the Ephesians by greeting them in the name of the Lord and blessing them. Paul says that we, as Christians, have all spiritual blessings that are offered through Jesus Christ. We are redeemed by the blood of Jesus and are called righteous in His sight. After you trusted and believed in the Lord Jesus Christ and were saved through Him, you were sealed with a promise. The promise is that you will receive an inheritance from the Lord. Paul goes on to pray for the believers that they will receive the spirit of wisdom and revelation from our heavenly Father, the Father of Jesus Christ, the Creator of the universe. After Jesus Christ was raised from the dead and He walked around on the earth for about forty days, He went back to His Father and was seated at His right hand in heavenly places. He was seated far above all rulers, powers, and every name because His name is above every name. It is by grace that we, as Christians, have been saved. God had grace upon us and sent His one and only Son to die for us. Paul tells the Ephesians that the love of God passes all knowledge, and we should know the heights and depths of the love that He has for us. He is able to do so much more for us than we can even think or imagine because of His great power that dwells within us as Christians.

Something new that I learned today was:

Ephesians 1:18 (NKJV) " The eyes of your understanding being enlightened; that you may know what is the hope of His calling, what are the riches of the glory of His inheritance in the saints."

Write and Draw Box

Unit 3: Lesson 110

Lesson Focus: Paul talks to the Ephesians

Opening prayer...

Bible Verse

Ephesians 1:18 (NKJV) " The eyes of your understanding being enlightened; that you may know what is the hope of His calling, what are the riches of the glory of His inheritance in the saints."

What do you already know?

What do you want to know?

Bible Lesson

Paul starts off chapter 4 in Ephesians by saying that he is a prisoner of Jesus Christ. Paul was in prison for many years for preaching the gospel of Jesus Christ. When Paul was called by God to preach, and he had the vision from Jesus, Ananias was told by the Lord that Paul would suffer many things in the name of Jesus. Paul also says that the Ephesian Christians should bear with one another in love, gentleness, and longsuffering. Longsuffering just means patience towards someone else. Paul starts talking about the different callings of the believer. They are: "He Himself gave some to be apostles, some prophets, some evangelists, and some pastors and teachers, 12 for the equipping of the saints for the work of ministry, for the edifying of the body of Christ." (Ephesians 4:11-12 NKJV) Apostles are people who are leaders over many churches or other leaders who are sent by God. This person could also possibly be called a church planter. Prophets are those who can speak the future or a message by hearing from the Lord. Evangelists are those who purposefully go out to share the good news of Jesus Christ with others and challenge them to accept Christ as their Savior. Pastors are leaders of a group of believers who help the believers grow in Christ, and the word pastor means shepherd. Think of a shepherd watching over his sheep, and a pastor does the same thing for his people. Teachers are those who teach the Word of God to others so that they can grow in Christ and in their knowledge of the Word of God.

Something new that I learned today was:

Ephesians 1:18 (NKJV) " The eyes of your understanding being enlightened; that you may know what is the hope of His calling, what are the riches of the glory of His inheritance in the saints."

Write and Draw Box

Unit 3: Lesson 111

Lesson Focus: Paul talks to the Philippians

Opening prayer...

Bible Verse

Philippians 2:3 (NKJV) "Let nothing be done through selfish ambition or conceit, but in lowliness of mind let each esteem others better than himself."

What do you already know?

What do you want to know?

Bible Lesson

Paul greets the people of Philippi by telling them that he has been praying for them and and that He who has begun a good work in them will complete it until the day of Jesus Christ. As Paul talked to the Philippians, he says that he is in chains and that while he is in chains, he is thinking about and praying for them. Paul says that by life or by death, we will serve the Lord. If it is by living, then we will have fruit from our labor, and if it is by death, then Christ will be glorified through death. Either way, we should live our days here on the earth as if we are living that day only. The Bible says that our life is like a mist; we are here today, and then we are gone tomorrow. In light of all of eternity, this life that we live here on the earth is just a very brief dot on the timeline of eternity. Whatever we do here on the earth, we should make it count for His glory. Our conduct here on the earth should be worthy of the gospel of Jesus Christ. We should work together in the faith of the gospel and have love for each other. We should not be selfish or vain in what we do, not looking only to our own interests but to the interests of others. Jesus made Himself nothing and took the form of a servant when He came down to the earth so that we could have an example to follow. We should also serve each other just as Christ came to serve. God the Father exalted Jesus to the highest position when He went back to the Father and gave Him the name above every name. In the name of Jesus, every knee will bow, and every tongue will confess that He is Lord of all.

Something new that I learned today was:

Philippians 2:3 (NKJV) "Let nothing be done through selfish ambition or conceit, but in lowliness of mind let each esteem others better than himself."

Write and Draw Box

Unit 3: Lesson 112

Lesson Focus: Paul talks to the Philippians

Opening prayer...

Bible Verse

Philippians 2:3 (NKJV) "Let nothing be done through selfish ambition or conceit, but in lowliness of mind let each esteem others better than himself."

What do you already know?

What do you want to know?

Bible Lesson

Paul says to the Philippians that we should do everything without complaining and arguing. We should be blameless and harmless children of God. We should shine like a light to others, and they will see that something is different about us. He says to the Philippians that they should beware of people who are evil workers but be confident in Jesus Christ and not in their own flesh. Paul talks again about his suffering for Christ and how he has lost everything, but he counts all those losses and trials as garbage. All the things of this world will soon disappear, and only the things we do for Christ will matter for eternity. We do not do things in our own righteousness but through the righteousness of God in Christ Jesus. He says that we do not look to those things that are behind us. We look forward towards Jesus Christ, pressing on towards the prize that is waiting for us in Christ Jesus. There are many enemies of the cross of Christ, and we should understand that we are not citizens of this world. Still, we await our return to our heavenly home, where Jesus Christ is waiting for us. There is no time in heaven like there is on earth, and we will live in heaven for all of eternity when it is our time to go and meet Jesus. While we are here on the earth, we must occupy our time and work for the Lord, and take as many people with us to heaven as we can. Jesus awaits us in heaven, and He values you deeply as His child.

Something new that I learned today was:

Philippians 2:3 (NKJV) "Let nothing be done through selfish ambition or conceit, but in lowliness of mind let each esteem others better than himself."

Write and Draw Box

Unit 3 Week 28: Assessment

Lesson Focus: Ephesians/Philippians

Opening prayer...

Bible Verse: Write or tell the Bible verse to your parent.

Philippians 2:3 (NKJV)

"Let _____ be done through _____ ambition or conceit, but in lowliness of mind let each esteem others better than himself."

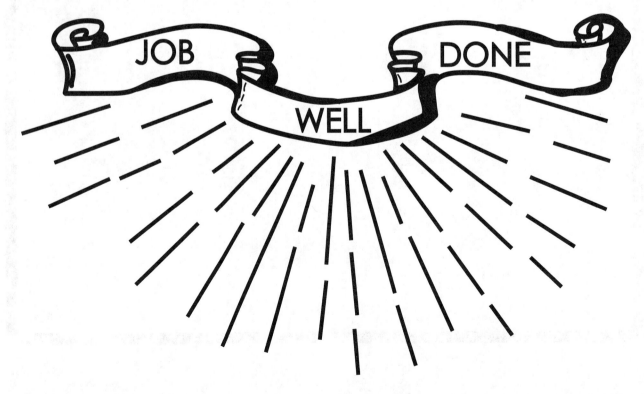

Write, draw or tell your parents what you learned this week. Talk about your favorite things.

Unit 3: Lesson 113

Lesson Focus: Paul talks to Timothy

Opening prayer...

Bible Verse

I Timothy 4:12 (NKJV) "Let no one despise your youth, but be an example to the believers in word, in conduct, in love, in spirit, in faith, in purity."

What do you already know?

What do you want to know?

Bible Lesson

Paul is instructing Timothy about some of the things that he has seen going on among the believers. He addresses his letter by calling Timothy a true son in the faith. It is thought that Timothy was trained by Paul, and they were very close. That is why Paul calls him his son in the faith. Paul warns of people teaching false doctrine and that believers in the Way should not adhere to these false teachings. Some had turned away from the faith and followed after these false teachings, so this is why Paul was warning about it. Then Paul shares how he used to be a <u>blasphemer</u>, <u>persecutor</u>, and <u>arrogant</u> man until God got ahold of him and changed his heart and beliefs through His great mercy. Paul talks about some people he turned over to satan because they rejected the faith in good <u>conscience</u>. He starts talking about believers praying for those in authority over them like kings, because it is good and acceptable in the sight of the Lord. His desire was for all to come to the knowledge and understanding that Jesus Christ is the Mediator between God the Father and man. He also goes on to talk about some of the ways that men and women can stay pure before the Lord. Dressing correctly and not causing others to stumble and fall is one of the things he mentions to the believers and Timothy.

Something new that I learned today was:

I Timothy 4:12 (NKJV) "Let no one despise your youth, but be an example to the believers in word, in conduct, in love, in spirit, in faith, in purity."

Write and Draw Box

Unit 3: Lesson 114

Lesson Focus: Paul talks to Timothy

Opening prayer...

Bible Verse

I Timothy 4:12 (NKJV) "Let no one despise your youth, but be an example to the believers in word, in conduct, in love, in spirit, in faith, in purity."

What do you already know?

What do you want to know?

Bible Lesson

Paul starts talking about the qualifications that the overseers and deacons should have if they are going to be leaders of the believers. Paul said that he had hoped to come and visit the believers soon. Still, if he could not, he wanted them to know how they should conduct themselves properly among other believers in the house of God. The church of Jesus Christ is the pillar of truth, so believers should gather together to teach and train each other in the Lord. Many follow after the doctrines of demons and try to persuade others to stray away from the truth of the word of God as well. Paul also instructs the believers with what he learned from Peter, that every creature of God is good, and nothing is to be refused if it is done with thanksgiving to the Lord. This is talking about foods, because Paul followed after a religion that did not eat certain foods before he followed after Christ. He wanted to make sure to train the believers in the truth that he had received from a disciple of Jesus Christ. Paul talks to Timothy and says, "Let no one despise your youth, but be an example to the believers in word, in conduct, in love, in spirit, in faith, in purity." (I Timothy 4:12 NKJV) He talks about believers honoring widows and those who are elders in the church. Today, we need to take note of these teachings from Paul and make sure that we also honor those who are widows and elders over us.

Something new that I learned today was:

I Timothy 4:12 (NKJV) "Let no one despise your youth, but be an example to the believers in word, in conduct, in love, in spirit, in faith, in purity."

Write and Draw Box

Unit 3: Lesson 115

Lesson Focus: Hebrews

Opening prayer...

Bible Verse
Hebrews 2:18 (NKJV)
"For in that He Himself has suffered, being tempted, He is able to aid those who are tempted."

What do you already know?

What do you want to know?

Bible Lesson

In the past, God spoke to the fathers of old by the prophets. Today, we have Jesus Christ, who speaks to us by His Spirit. We can come before Father God, the Creator of the universe, only by the blood of His Son Jesus Christ. Jesus, when He came to the earth as a man, was made like us, and He was tempted as we are so that He can help us when we are tempted. Jesus died for us so that He can have victory over death and the grave. Just as God the Father created the world as we know it and rested on the last day, we should enter into rest as well. The author of Hebrews goes on to say in chapter 4 verse 12, "For the word of God is living and powerful, and sharper than any two-edged sword, piercing even to the division of soul and spirit, and of joints and marrow, and is a discerner of the thoughts and intents of the heart." (NKJV) We must understand that the word of God is powerful, and it is alive and active. We can read the Bible over and over again, and God can still reveal something new to us each and every time. One day soon, we will all stand before our Creator and give account for everything we have done and could have done while we were here on this earth. There is no condemnation for those who are in Christ Jesus. That day will not be a day when we will be condemned by Him, but we will see our obedience to Him. All of our sins will be covered by the blood of Jesus and will be remembered no more. Jesus was tempted just like we are, and yet He did not sin. He is our example, and we can come before His throne of grace to find mercy and forgiveness each and every day.

Something new that I learned today was:

Hebrews 2:18 (NKJV) "For in that He Himself has suffered, being tempted, He is able to aid those who are tempted."

Write and Draw Box

Unit 3: Lesson 116

Lesson Focus: Hebrews

Opening prayer...

Bible Verse
Hebrews 2:18 (NKJV)
"For in that He Himself has suffered, being tempted, He is able to aid those who are tempted."

What do you already know?

What do you want to know?

Bible Lesson

The writer of Hebrews tells them that they should be eating the solid food of the word, but they are still having the milk of the word. In other words, they have not moved into maturity yet in the things of the Lord. The author says that the Lord is our High Priest, and He is making intercession for us. Jesus, our Lord, came from the lineage of the tribe of Judah, which is where the order of high priests comes from. Since Jesus will never die, He is our high priest forever, and He always lives to make intercession for us. We can go before Him and be cleansed, because He has offered Himself up as a sacrifice for us once and for all. He is seated at the right hand of the heavenly Father, and every high priest must offer something to the Father as a sacrifice. Jesus offered up Himself for us, and He is the Mediator between God the Father and man. The author goes on to say, "For this is the covenant that I will make with the house of Israel after those days, says the LORD: I will put My laws in their mind and write them on their hearts, and I will be their God, and they shall be My people." (Hebrews 8:10 NKJV) The Hebrew people have been looking for the Messiah for thousands of years. When Jesus was on the earth, they rejected Him as the Messiah because He was the son of the carpenter Joseph, whom they knew. They did not know that Jesus was given to Mary by the Holy Spirit, and that He was and is God's Son. God says that they will be my people, and I will write my law on their hearts. Jesus entered the most holy place, not with the blood of bulls and goats like other priests, but He entered it with His blood and offered Himself as the final sacrifice for all.

Something new that I learned today was:

Hebrews 2:18 (NKJV) "For in that He Himself has suffered, being tempted, He is able to aid those who are tempted."

Write and Draw Box

Unit 3 Week 29: Assessment

Lesson Focus: Timothy / Hebrews

Opening prayer...

Bible Verse: Write or tell the Bible verse to your parent.

Hebrews 2:18 (NKJV)

"For in that He _____ has

_____, being tempted, He

is able to aid those who are tempted."

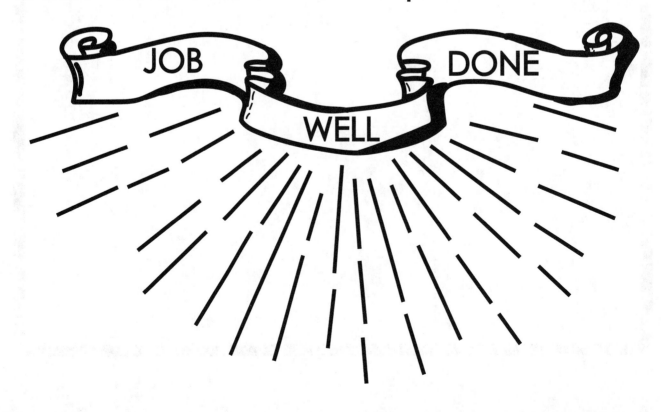

Write, draw or tell your parents what you learned this week. Talk about your favorite things.

Unit 3: Lesson 117

Lesson Focus: James

Opening prayer...

Bible Verse
James 1:2+3 (NKJV)
"My brethren, count it all joy when you fall into various trials, 3 knowing that the testing of your faith produces patience."

What do you already know?

What do you want to know?

Bible Lesson

James starts by stating that we should count it joy if we have trials and tests because they produce patience in us. If we lack wisdom, we should ask God, and He will give us wisdom. When we ask, we should not doubt but have faith that what we ask for will be done for us. We should not be like the waves of the sea that toss back and forth, and we should not doubt in our hearts, or we will be unstable in all that we do. He also goes on toshare about how Christians can earn a crown of life when enduring temptation. This crown of life is a promise to us from God the Father. When we are tempted to do things that we should not do, we should not say that we are tempted by God, because God does not tempt us. On the other hand, when we are tempted, we should not give into the desires of the flesh because when we do, we are led into sin by giving into those temptations. The devil even tempted Jesus in the desert, but what did Jesus do to fight off the temptations of the devil? He used the scriptures to fight against the enemy. The Bible says every good and perfect gift is from above. We should not hurry to speak; we should be slow to speak and slow to get angry with others. We should set aside all evil desires and follow after Christ, who helps us in our weakness. We need to stay in the word of God daily to fight off the enemy when he comes to tempt us like he tempted Jesus in the desert. Jesus used scripture to defeat every temptation and attack.

Something new that I learned today was:

James 1:2+3 (NKJV) " My brethren, count it all joy when you fall into various trials, 3 knowing that the testing of your faith produces patience."

Write and Draw Box

Unit 3: Lesson 118

Lesson Focus: James

Opening prayer...

Bible Verse
James 1:2+3 (NKJV)
"My brethren, count it all joy when you fall into various trials, 3 knowing that the testing of your faith produces patience."

What do you already know?

What do you want to know?

Bible Lesson

James says that we should be doers of the word and not just hearers of the word. When we hear the word and do not act upon it, we are like a man looking in a mirror who looks away and forgets what he looks like. The lesson is that when we hear and read the scriptures, we need to act on what the word says, not just read and listen to it. Everyone who thinks they are religious but does not tame their tongue is only deceiving themselves, and their religion is useless. The scripture tells us what pure religion is. It says that pure religion, according to the Father, is to visit and take care of orphans and widows, and keep ourselves from the world. James goes on to say that we are not to show partiality towards others. If a man in nice clothes and a man in poor-looking clothes comes to you, a person is not to show favoritism to a person that is dressed nicely. The Bible says that we are to love our neighbor as ourselves, and we are not to show favoritism. If someone has faith but does not have works, then what good is it? If someone comes to you that needs clothing and you send them away without clothing, what good is your faith? So, faith without works is dead. James also says that not many of the believers there should be teachers because teachers will have a stricter judgment. A person's tongue is like the rudder of a ship that needs to be controlled; otherwise, it can get out of control quickly. Even though your tongue is a small part of your body, it is powerful. The words that we speak have the power of life and death. Choose the words that you speak wisely and speak life to others.

Something new that I learned today was:

James 1:2+3 (NKJV) " My brethren, count it all joy when you fall into various trials, 3 knowing that the testing of your faith produces patience."

Write and Draw Box

Unit 3: Lesson 119

Lesson Focus: Peter

Opening prayer...

Bible Verse

I Peter 2:24 (NKJV) "Who Himself bore our sins in His own body on the tree, that we, having died to sins, might live for righteousness by whose stripes you were healed."

What do you already know?

What do you want to know?

Bible Lesson

Peter begins his letter by greeting those who are at the different churches. Then he says that they should not give in to their former sinful desires that they once had. Peter encourages them to be holy like the Lord as it is written in the Old Testament, "Be ye holy as I am holy." The Lord judges each person's work without showing favoritism, and we were not redeemed with things that will pass away like gold and silver, but through the precious blood of Jesus Christ. Jesus was a lamb without any fault, which is important when offering a sacrifice before God the Father. If a lamb had a spot or blemish on it, it could not be used as an acceptable sacrifice before the Lord. Jesus was perfect in all that he did, and he did not sin. That is why when He died for us as a sinless sacrifice, it was once and for all. No other sacrifices need to be made because Jesus paid it all for us. God the Father raised Jesus from the dead and seated Him at His right hand in heaven and gave Him the name that is above every name. Because of this, we as Christians are to love each other with a pure heart because the living word of God lives within us as believers. Peter tells the believers that they are to flee from evil desires like those who are just new in the faith, who still need the milk of the word of God, and not the meat. Believers are to grow in Christ and not just stay on the basic teachings of Christ, but continually read and study the word of God so that you can grow spiritually in Him.

Something new that I learned today was:

I Peter 2:24 (NKJV) "Who Himself bore our sins in His own body on the tree, that we, having died to sins, might live for righteousness by whose stripes you were healed."

Write and Draw Box

Unit 3: Lesson 120

Lesson Focus: Peter

Opening prayer...

Bible Verse

I Peter 2:24 (NKJV) "Who Himself bore our sins in His own body on the tree, that we, having died to sins, might live for righteousness by whose stripes you were healed."

What do you already know?

What do you want to know?

Bible Lesson

Peter encourages the believers by saying that they are a chosen generation, a royal priesthood, and God's own special people who have been called out of darkness and into the light. Flee from the <u>fleshly desires</u> that rise up within and behave acceptably to God the Father, being an example to others wherever you go. Believers are to submit to those in authority over them whether the one in authority over them is a believer or not. Those in authority are to be honored. When believers do good to others in the sight of the Lord, they silence the talk of foolish men. We must honor God, love people, and honor those who are in authority over us. Jesus was beaten for us and nailed to a cross so that we can be healed and saved. Just as Jesus still saves today, the same Jesus still heals today. If you or someone you know needs healing in their body, believe that Jesus took upon Himself a beating, so that you or they can be healed. God does not change, and we serve the same Jesus that walked around on this earth, went around healing everyone, and cast out devils. Jesus still heals, He still delivers, and He will continue to do these things until He comes back to take all the believers on earth to heaven with Him to rule and reign together forever. Just as Jesus Christ suffered for us, we must understand that if our Master suffered, we will also have suffering. But God will bring us through the suffering, and the Holy Spirit is always with us.

Something new that I learned today was:

I Peter 2:24 (NKJV) "Who Himself bore our sins in His own body on the tree, that we, having died to sins, might live for righteousness by whose stripes you were healed."

Write and Draw Box

Unit 3 Week 30: Assessment

Lesson Focus: James / Peter

Opening prayer...

Bible Verse: Write or tell the Bible verse to your parent.

I Peter 2:24 (NKJV) "Who Himself bore our
_____ in His own body
on the _____,
that we, having died to sins, might live for
righteousness by whose stripes you were
_____."

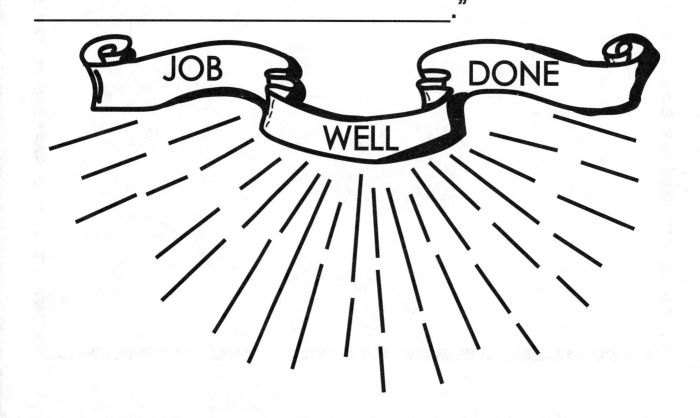

Write, draw or tell your parents what you learned this week. Talk about your favorite things.

Unit 3: Lesson 121

Lesson Focus: John

Opening prayer...

Bible Verse
I John 1:9 (NKJV)
"If we confess our sins, He is faithful and just to forgive us our sins and to cleanse us from all unrighteousness."

What do you already know?

What do you want to know?

Bible Lesson

John begins talking to those who would read his letter and saying that he has seen and witnessed Jesus Christ. He says that we have fellowship with the Father through Jesus Christ, and he is writing so that their joy may be full. God is light, and in Him, there is no darkness at all. If we walk with Him and have fellowship with Him, darkness has no place in us. The blood of Jesus cleanses us from all sin and unrighteousness. If we say that we do not have any sin, we are deceiving ourselves, and the truth is not within us. If we confess our sins to Him, He is faithful to us and forgives us from all our sins. John is writing this letter so that those who read it will not sin. He says that if you do sin, you have an <u>Advocate</u>, and His name is Jesus Christ. Jesus Christ not only died for our sins so that we can be forgiven, but He also died for all. Believers must keep the commands of God. If they do not keep His commands, they are liars, and the truth is not in them. The truth is not in anyone who claims to have the light in him and yet hates his brother. For those who love their brother, the light of the word is within them. Do not love the world or anything in the world. If anyone loves the world, the love of the Father is not in him. The word world here does not mean the earth, "the world" means things. It talks about things that nonbelievers do that are against what Jesus Christ would want them to do. Jesus continually told people to go and sin no more. As a believer in Jesus Christ, you are not to continue in sin. We must flee from sin and darkness. When we do sin, we have an Advocate who forgives us from all of our sins and cleanses us from all unrighteousness.

Something new that I learned today was:

I John 1:9 (NKJV) "If we confess our sins, He is faithful and just to forgive us our sins and to cleanse us from all unrighteousness."

Write and Draw Box

Unit 3: Lesson 122

Lesson Focus: John

Opening prayer...

Bible Verse
I John 1:9 (NKJV)
"If we confess our sins, He is faithful and just to forgive us our sins and to cleanse us from all unrighteousness."

What do you already know?

What do you want to know?

Bible Lesson

The world and what it wants and desires will pass away, but whoever does the will of the Father will live forever. John goes on to talk about when the antichrist will come and deceive many people. There will be many who claim to be the Christ during the last hours, but these will be false christs. Jesus Christ already came to us, died for our sins, will one day come back to get us riding on a white horse, and take us back to heaven with Him. Because believers in Jesus Christ have the truth in them, those who deny that Jesus was the Christ do not have the truth within them. A person who denies that Jesus was and is the Christ is an antichrist, and the truth is not in him. Some will try to lead people astray and claim that there are other christs, and we are not to believe such lies. These people who claim to be Christ may even do miracles, signs, and wonders, but they will not do these things in the name of Jesus Christ of Nazareth. They will do these things in the name of themselves or in the name of their father, satan. When Jesus Christ comes back for us, we will be like Him. We will be transformed in the blink of an eye. Do not let anyone lead you astray. Those who do good in the name of Jesus Christ of Nazareth belong to the Father, but those who do not do things in the name of Jesus Christ are from satan. The devil has been sinning from the beginning, and he is the father of all lies. Those who do not do what is right are not children of God, but those who do the will of the Father are called children of God.

Something new that I learned today was:

I John 1:9 (NKJV) "If we confess our sins, He is faithful and just to forgive us our sins and to cleanse us from all unrighteousness."

Write and Draw Box

Unit 3: Lesson 123

Lesson Focus: Revelation

Opening prayer...

Bible Verse

Revelation 3:20 (NKJV) " Behold, I stand at the door and knock. If anyone hears My voice and opens the door, I will come in to him and dine with him, and he with Me."

What do you already know?

What do you want to know?

Bible Lesson

The book of Revelation was given to John, who witnessed the life of Jesus. It says that the revelation is for things that will shortly take place. In heaven, time is not like it is here on the earth. The Bible even says in 2 Peter 3:8 that a day here on the earth is like a thousand years in heaven. After the greetings, John starts his letters to the seven churches in Asia. They teach that Jesus is coming back quickly, and we must be looking for His return. Jesus will return just like He left the earth. When the disciples were standing on the mountain with Him, He just started to go up into the sky, and then He disappeared. He will come back in the clouds, the Bible says. The Lord is the Beginning and the End, the one who was, who is, and who is to come. The Lord began to show John many things that are to come in the future. There is a lot of <u>symbolism</u> in the revelation that John received while he was on the island of Patmos. Lampstands, trumpets, and many other things <u>represent</u> things that we will see in the future. John tells the church at Ephesus that they must repent and turn from their evil ways. John says that they have left their first love. Our first love must be Jesus. Those who overcome evil while here on the earth will be able to eat of the tree of life, which is in heaven and in the presence of God.

Something new that I learned today was:

Revelation 3:20 (NKJV) " Behold, I stand at the door and knock. If anyone hears My voice and opens the door, I will come in to him and dine with him, and he with Me."

Write and Draw Box

Unit 3: Lesson 124

Lesson Focus: Revelation

Opening prayer...

Bible Verse

Revelation 3:20 (NKJV) "Behold, I stand at the door and knock. If anyone hears My voice and opens the door, I will come in to him and dine with him, and he with Me."

What do you already know?

What do you want to know?

Bible Lesson

To another one of the churches, John writes that they have been serving false gods. John continues to talk about repentance to these churches that have not been going after their first love, Jesus. They have been going after the things of the world, serving idols, and doing ungodly things in the sight of the Lord. The church of Philadelphia was a faithful church, John says, and they will receive the crown of life that is promised to us when we enter into the presence of the Lord. There was a lukewarm church, and the Lord says that He wishes that they were either hot or cold. Those who are lukewarm, the Lord will spit out of His mouth and not have any part with them. On the other hand, Jesus says that He stands at the door and knocks, and to those who open the door, He will come in and dine with them. Those who overcome will sit with Jesus on His throne because we are joint-heirs with Him. The passage describes the throne room of heaven and things that surround the throne of God. The throne is made out of beautiful stones and gems, and there are many beautiful creatures in the throne room worshiping their Creator. There is what looks like a sea of glass in front of the throne. This is where countless people in white robes wave palm branches worshiping the Savior. There are elders there as well, worshiping God and bowing down before the throne. What looks like lightning and thunder are coming from the throne of God. There will be a day of judgment for satan and all mankind. Everyone will stand before the Creator of the universe and give an account for their lives while here on the earth. We will stand there by ourselves, and we will see what we did for the Lord while here on the earth, and we will see what we could have done.

Something new that I learned today was:

Revelation 3:20 (NKJV) " Behold, I stand at the door and knock. If anyone hears My voice and opens the door, I will come in to him and dine with him, and he with Me."

Write and Draw Box

Unit 3 Week 31: Assessment

Lesson Focus: Revelation

Opening prayer...

Bible Verse: Write or tell the Bible verse to your parent.

Revelation 3:20 (NKJV) " Behold, I stand at the

_____ and knock. If anyone hears My

_____ and opens the door, I will

come in to him and dine with him, and he with Me."

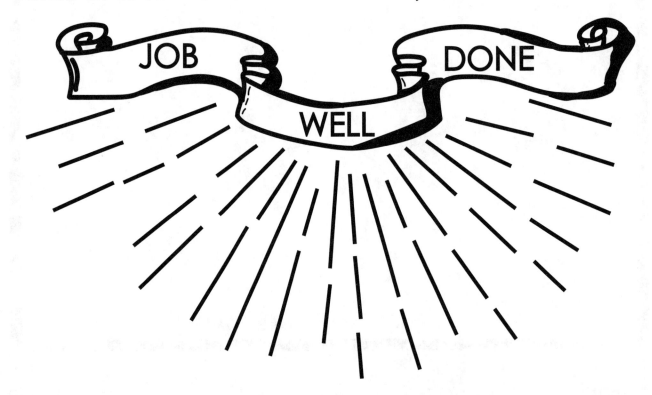

Write, draw or tell your parents what you learned this week. Talk about your favorite things.

Unit 3: Lesson 125

Lesson Focus: Birth of Jesus (Christmas)

Opening prayer...

Bible Verse

Luke 1:35 (NKJV) "The angel answered, "The Holy Spirit will come on you, and the power of the Most High will overshadow you. So the holy one to be born will be called the Son of God."

What do you already know?

What do you want to know?

Bible Lesson

Mary and Joseph, Jesus' earthly parents, promised each other that they would get married. This is called a pledge. An angel of the Lord came to Mary in the night and greeted her as the one who is highly favored. Mary did not know what to think of the angel's words to her. The angel told her that the Holy Spirit would overshadow her, and she would have a baby boy who would be called the Son of the Most High God. The angel told her that the boy's name would be Jesus, and that the Lord would give Him the throne of His father David. He would rule and reign forever because His kingdom would never end. Mary did something so very powerful; she said to the angel, "May your word to me be fulfilled." This means that Mary was obedient to God the Father without hesitation. We need to do this ourselves as well. When the Lord speaks, we must listen and obey. When it came time for the baby Jesus to be born, Mary and Joseph were traveling. They were traveling because there was something called a census happening in the land. This is where the government counts all of the people and makes sure that everyone pays their taxes. This is why everywhere that they went, the places to stay were full. Mary and Joseph ended up staying in an animal stable that night when Jesus was born. Many angels, shepherds, and wise men would visit them to worship the newborn King. They brought gifts to King Jesus. They brought gold, frankincense, and myrrh; gifts fit for a King. This is the actual reason that we celebrate Christmas. We celebrate the birth of our Savior, Jesus Christ. May we never forget that this is the real reason we celebrate and give gifts like they did that day, so many years ago. Give gifts to your King today. Offer up praise to Him and tell Him that you will serve Him all the days of your life.

Something new that I learned today was:

Luke 1:35 (NKJV) "The angel answered, "The Holy Spirit will come on you, and the power of the Most High will overshadow you. So the holy one to be born will be called the Son of God."

Write and Draw Box

Unit 3: Lesson 126

Lesson Focus: Jesus' triumphal entry (Palm Sunday)

Opening prayer...

Bible Verse

Matthew 21:9 (NKJV) The crowds that went ahead of him and those that followed shouted, "Hosanna to the Son of David! Blessed is he who comes in the name of the Lord! Hosanna in the highest heaven!"

What do you already know?

What do you want to know?

Bible Lesson

Jesus and His disciples were heading towards Jerusalem, and Jesus told two of them to go on ahead of them and find a donkey tied up in the next village. Jesus also said to them, "When you see the donkey tell the owner that the Master is in need of it, and they will give it to you." They did just as Jesus had told them, and they brought the donkey back to Jesus. Jesus got up on the donkey and rode into Jerusalem just like any earthly king would enter into a city. Many people there spread out their coats and waved palm branches saying, "Hosanna to the Son of David! Blessed is He who comes in the name of the Lord! Hosanna in the highest heaven!" (Matthew 21:9 NKJV) The disciples and followers of Jesus really thought that Jesus would come into Jerusalem and take over as the new earthly king. During this time in history, Rome had taken over the area, and the local people wanted to have a king again. It was really looking like Jesus would be the people's next king. After all, Jesus was from the lineage of King David, and He did have the right to claim the throne. Jesus has a kingdom that the people did not know and understand about. He told Herod that His kingdom was not of this world, and he was right when he called Him a King. Someday, Jesus will come back to the earth, and we will rule and reign with Him. He is King Jesus!

Something new that I learned today was:

Matthew 21:9 (NKJV) The crowds that went ahead of him and those that followed shouted, "Hosanna to the Son of David! Blessed is he who comes in the name of the Lord! Hosanna in the highest heaven!"

Write and Draw Box

Unit 3: Lesson 127

Lesson Focus: Christ's crucifixion and resurrection
(Resurrection Sunday)

Opening prayer...

Bible Verse
Matthew 28:6 (NKJV)

"He is not here; for He is risen, as He said. Come, see the place where the Lord lay."

What do you already know?

What do you want to know?

Bible Lesson

It was early in the morning on the first day of the week, three days after Jesus was crucified on a cross. The Bible says that Jesus took upon Himself the sins of the world. Because of this, Jesus was separated from His Father for the first time ever. This is why Jesus cried out on the cross, "My God, My God, why have you forsaken me?" (Matthew 27:46 NKJV) Where God is, there is no sin or darkness. Jesus went into the pit of hell to suffer for three days for all mankind. When Mary Magdalene went to the tomb that morning, she saw that the covering had been rolled away. An angel stood there and said to her, "Do not be afraid, for I know that you seek Jesus who was crucified. 6 He is not here; for He is risen, as He said. Come, see the place where the Lord lay." (Matthew 28:5-6 NKJV) Mary went in and looked where Jesus was laid, and He was not there just as the angel had said. Mary ran to tell the disciples the news. When she was on her way to tell them, Jesus appeared to her. Jesus told her to tell the disciples to go to Galilee and wait for Him there. As they were doing this, some of the guards went into the city and told the chief priests what had happened. The chief priests paid the guards, and told them to tell people that the disciples had stolen the body of Jesus. Jesus met the disciples in Galilee, and some there still did not believe that it was Jesus. He was risen from the dead, just as He said that He would. He told the disciples that all authority had been given to Him, and now He was giving this authority to them. We have this same authority from Jesus today. He tells us to go and preach the good news, cast out demons, heal the sick, and raise the dead. Freely we have received, we should freely give.

Something new that I learned today was:

Matthew 28:6 (NKJV) "He is not here; for He is risen, as He said. Come, see the place where the Lord lay."

Write and Draw Box

Unit 3: Lesson 128

Jesus is alive, and He returns to heaven (The Day of Pentecost and the sending of the promised Holy Spirit)

Opening prayer...

Bible Verse
Matthew 28:6 (NKJV)

"He is not here; for He is risen, as He said. Come, see the place where the Lord lay."

What do you already know?

What do you want to know?

Bible Lesson

Jesus met with His disciples after He had risen from the dead, and He told them that they must go and preach the good news of the gospel of Jesus Christ to all nations. He told them they must go to Jerusalem and wait for the Holy Spirit to come upon them. Right in front of their eyes, Jesus is taken up into heaven and is now seated at the right hand of His Father. The disciples did exactly what Jesus had told them, and they headed for Jerusalem. While there, they were praying, and a mighty rushing wind filled the place, and what looked like fire rested on each of them as they spoke in other tongues. They were filled with the Spirit, and those who were there in the city were from all different regions and spoke different languages. As the disciples were filled with the Spirit and spoke in other tongues, many that were there visiting could hear them speaking in their own language. Peter stood up and spoke from from the Old Testament scriptures and told the people there that this was prophesied long ago, that the Lord would pour out His Spirit on all flesh. "Your sons and your daughters shall prophesy, your young men shall see visions, your old men shall dream dreams." (Joel 2 NKJV) Believe this for yourself today. You will prophesy, and you will see visions in the mighty name of Jesus.

Something new that I learned today was:

Matthew 28:6 (NKJV) "He is not here; for He is risen, as He said. Come, see the place where the Lord lay."

Write and Draw Box